KNOW YOUR RIGHTS

and

CLAIM THEM

'We can stand up for our rights once we understand them. This book is a guide for every child and young person who believes in liberty, equality and a better world for all'
MALALA YOUSAFZAI

'Children are the future. This is the perfect book for young people who care about the world and want to make a difference'
GRETA THUNBERG

KNOW YOUR YOUR RIGHTS

and
CLAIM THEM

Written by Nicky Parker
at Amnesty International
with Angelina Jolie
and Geraldine Van Bueren QC

ANDERSEN PRESS

First published in 2021 by
Andersen Press Limited
20 Vauxhall Bridge Road, London SW1V 2SA, UK
Vijverlaan 48, 3062 HL, Rotterdam, Nederland
www.andersenpress.co.uk

2 4 6 8 10 9 7 5 3 1

British Library Cataloguing in Publication Data available.

ISBN 978 1 83913 119 6

Printed and bound in Great Britain by Clays Ltd, Elcograf S.p.A.

This book has complex ideas
and can be emotionally
challenging. You may find
it best to read it in stages,
taking time to reflect or
discuss it with others before
resuming. Or you could
consult it as and when you
need to. If it motivates you
to take action, first check if
it is safe for you to do so.

Words highlighted in bold in
this book are explained in
Useful Terms on p251.

PART THREE: CLAIM YOUR RIGHTS

PART FOUR: RESOURCES AND OTHER INFORMATION

FOREWORD BY ANGELINA JOLIE

Here's a truth you may not know:

As a young person, your rights have equal status to the rights of an adult.

Not when you reach adulthood, or leave home, or get your first job, but *now*.

Whoever you are, wherever you live, no matter your race, ethnicity, religion or gender, or if you are rich or poor, your life is of equal value to any adult, or any other young person on the planet.

No one has the right to harm you, to silence you, to tell you what to think or believe, to treat you as if you don't matter, or to prevent you from participating fully in society. No one has the right to deny you knowledge of your rights.

That is not just my opinion. It is set out in a legally-binding international agreement – the UN Convention on the Rights of the Child – signed by 196 countries. It means your rights have the force of law.

If governments kept their word, and if all adults respected children's rights, there would be no need for this book.

But there is a huge gap between your rights as a child in principle, and what happens in practice.

In fact, there will be some adults who won't want you to read this book at all. They may come up with all sorts of reasons to argue why child rights don't apply to you, or to your country. This book will arm you with knowledge to help you defend your rights or the rights of others.

It explains how child rights came into being, and were put in place with your safety and individual growth in mind.

It describes how your rights work in practice, and the reality of situations in which they are ignored.

It includes chapters on how to develop your skills as an activist, how to exercise your right to peaceful protest – safely – and how to think about your digital security.

And it contains accounts of young people who have successfully claimed their rights, changing the way governments or their communities treat children. These stories show that every act, no matter how small, can make a difference. When young people join together, you have a moral power and physical presence no one can ignore.

So I hope this book will help you to identify who or what stands between you and your rights, and the action you can take if you choose. I hope it will inspire you to know your rights – and claim them.

Angelina Jolie, October 2020

PART ONE
KNOW YOUR RIGHTS

'It is better to
light a candle
than curse the
darkness.'

Chinese proverb, and the motto of
Amnesty International

YOUR RIGHTS

If you are a child or a young person, you have your own set of human rights. Child rights are human rights especially designed for children and young people. You have had them since the moment you were born. You will have them until you reach what is called 'the **age of majority**', which in most countries is eighteen years old.

They are precious freedoms and protections, your own set of laws. They exist to look after you, to help you flourish, and so your voice can be heard. They are part of a body of international human rights, to which you are entitled because you are human.

Child rights are positive. They aspire to the very best for all children and young people, everywhere.

They are yours, no matter who you are or where you live. Whatever your gender, sexuality, gender identity, race, ethnicity, colour, faith or culture, whether you're rich or poor, disabled or non-disabled, neurodiverse or neurotypical, living with your own family, in a care home, on the streets or in a refugee camp, these rights belong to you. Equally. No one has more or fewer child rights than anyone else.

Your rights are **inalienable**. This means that no one is allowed to take them away from you. But be aware: you may face many attempts to deny you your rights.

Your rights can be upheld by law. But they need defending. There will be those who think they would be better off if you had fewer rights. They may try to **violate** or **abuse** them. Governments and other authorities are supposed to step in and help you, but they don't always do this.

Some legal language: states and governments violate rights. Individuals and companies abuse them. The term abuser is also used for someone who tries to control you in an intimate or sexual way.

You may hear some people say that human rights are dangerous, too political or inappropriate for children to know, or that they are foreign imports. This isn't true. Rights are beneficial and they are yours, regardless of anyone's politics or beliefs. The danger comes when they are not respected.

You are a rights holder. You need to know what your rights are so you can stand up for them, for yourself and others. Standing up for others is also called **solidarity**. In essence, solidarity is a value, a shared sense of humanity, that enables people to connect with others and support them, no matter their differences.

This book is a manual for you to know, understand and claim your rights.

WHO IS A CHILD?

The law considers you a child until you reach the 'age of majority'. That is the threshold of adulthood, when you become accountable in the eyes of the law and can vote in local and often national elections. It may also be the age at which you can get married, have a driving licence and work, although these vary between countries. In most places, you reach the age of majority when you turn eighteen, which is what the United Nations **Committee on the Rights of the Child** recommends (see page 22 for more information about the Committee). Some countries, like Austria and Brazil, have changed the regulations to give you more of a voice, enabling you to vote in national elections when you are sixteen, though you are still legally a child entitled to child rights and protections. In Iran, however, boys reach the age of majority at fifteen lunar years, while for girls it is nine lunar years. This means that Iran's laws do not protect children and young people for as long – for example, child marriage can be forced on girls as young as nine. Much is determined by cultural norms in your country. These can bring advantages and disadvantages to you as an individual, but it's also worth reflecting on how these norms benefit those in authority.

As a teenager, you may be a young person nearing adulthood, but in the eyes of the law you have child rights. When you become an adult, you will still have human rights – just not child rights.

There are about 2.3 billion children in the world, nearly a third of the total human population. Make the most of your rights. Know them and claim them.

Oppression is a power system that keeps privilege for those in dominant groups. It takes place on many different levels across society. On a *personal* level, for example, someone may carry beliefs about others based on class, race or gender; they might not articulate these beliefs, but they still affect their opinions and actions. On an *interpersonal* level, someone's beliefs might make them treat others as if they are less important. On an *institutional* level, there are often rules and policies (written and unwritten) that exclude people or stop them feeling welcome. At the *cultural* level, oppressive beliefs are sent out far and wide on a daily basis through the media, books, government announcements and so on. They are part of shaping widespread views that can make people accept oppression unthinkingly. It becomes a vicious circle.

A SHORT HISTORY OF CHILD RIGHTS

Human rights are laws that are rooted in globally accepted ethical values, such as equality, dignity and justice. They are how you expect to be treated as a person. Human rights provide a structure of agreed rules that protect you from oppression and abuse of power. They are informed by the moral teachings of most faiths and cultural traditions.

Child rights give you extra protection as a child or young person. They come to you mainly (but not only) through the United Nations Convention on the Rights of the Child of 1989.

WHEN CHILDREN (AND MOST ADULTS) HAD NO RIGHTS

All human rights have been hard-won. People have fought and died for them for hundreds of years.

In 539 BCE, Cyrus the Great, the first king of ancient Persia, issued what may be the earliest **charter** of human rights. He ordered slaves to be freed, stated that everyone had the right to choose their own religion and said that people of all races were equal.

His decrees were recorded on a baked-clay cylinder in the Akkadian language with cuneiform script, now known as the Cyrus Cylinder.

The idea of human rights spread quickly to India, Greece and eventually Rome. The following centuries saw the rise of more documents asserting rights, such as Magna Carta (Great Charter) in 1215, which embedded some rights into English law. It excluded most ordinary people but influenced later human rights law.

Throughout history, many adults and children did not enjoy rights. Most families were very poor and needed their children to bring in food and money.

Large numbers of children laboured from the age of three in fields, at home and, later, in factories. They were hungry, exhausted and uneducated. Malnutrition stunted the growth of many. Lack of education and play made it impossible to develop properly.

From the 18th century, activists in different countries began to campaign for child rights, and against terrible working conditions. They argued that the **state** (meaning local and national governments) had a duty to step in and protect vulnerable children, and that children had a right to be educated. New laws were made because of these campaigns. They included the UK's Factory Act of 1833, which banned using children under the age of nine in factories. In 1881, India's Factory Act outlawed the employment of children under seven.

Gradually, attitudes towards children began to change around the world. Campaigners pushed hard for the right to education because they knew it could help unlock a child's potential. The United States introduced free primary education for all children by 1870. Two years later, Japan did the same. By the end of the 19th century, children in many developed countries were given free primary education.

THE RISE OF HUMAN RIGHTS

In the first quarter of the 20th century, World War One claimed about 16 million lives in over thirty countries. The global influenza pandemic that immediately followed killed another 50 million. Huge numbers of children were orphaned.

> '**All wars, whether just or unjust, disastrous or victorious, are waged against the child.**'
>
> *Eglantyne Jebb, 1919*

Campaigners were deeply concerned for the welfare of children. In 1924 they achieved the first ever international child rights charter – the Geneva Declaration of the Rights of the Child. This was drafted by Eglantyne Jebb, who also founded the Save the Children Fund. The main aim of the Declaration was to give children the essentials for survival and development: food, healthcare, education, clean water and help in times of need. It was a real step forward. But it still viewed children as less capable beings who were unable to speak for themselves.

A few years later came World War Two, the deadliest

military conflict in history. It caused the deaths of about 75 million people between 1939 and 1945. On one side were Germany, Italy and Japan, known as the Axis powers; on the other were the Allied forces, including the United States, Great Britain, the Soviet Union, France and China.

'Children are not the people of tomorrow, but people today. They are entitled to be taken seriously. They have a right to be treated by adults with tenderness and respect, as equals. They should be allowed to grow into whoever they were meant to be – the unknown person inside each of them is our hope for the future.'

Janusz Korczak, 1927, educator and child rights campaigner who chose not to save himself but marched with Jewish orphans into Treblinka death camp.

Many of the millions of deaths were caused by the **Holocaust**, carried out by the German Nazi party and their collaborators in European countries. This was a **genocide**, the deliberate mass killing of an entire group of people in the attempt to wipe them out of existence. During the Holocaust the Nazis murdered six million

Jewish people across the entire continent of Europe, including about 1.5 million children. They also killed people with disabilities, gay people, Gypsy, Roma and Sinti people, anyone who opposed them politically (mainly communists, trade unionists and social democrats), as well as people whose religious beliefs conflicted with their ideology.

> Anne Frank was a Jewish girl who in 1942 went into hiding with her family during the Nazi occupation of the Netherlands. Two years later they were discovered, and captured by the Nazis. In 1945 Anne died in the inhumane conditions of the Bergen-Belsen **concentration camp**. Anne wrote a world-famous diary about her thoughts and experiences, which has contributed to much greater awareness of the dangers of **discrimination** like **anti-Semitism**. She wrote, 'How wonderful it is that nobody need wait a single moment before starting to improve the world.'

Many other deaths were caused by intensive aerial bombing raids carried out by both sides. Allied forces' bombing raids, for example, killed about 410,000 German civilians and destroyed entire cities, from Berlin to Hamburg. German bombing raids known as 'the Blitz' killed nearly 40,000 British people (including over 5,000 children) in just eight months between 1940 and 1941.

Germany surrendered in May 1945 but the war continued in Asia. In August that year, US forces dropped two nuclear bombs on the Japanese cities of Hiroshima and Nagasaki. At least 214,000 people died, including thousands of children. Japan surrendered soon after, ending the war.

After the war, world leaders came together in the United Nations to say 'never again'. For the first time they agreed on global human rights that would help to prevent atrocities. In 1948 the Universal Declaration of Human Rights (UDHR) was born. It was truly radical. It offered hope and a lifetime of legal protection to everyone from birth to death. It gave people a powerful legal tool to fight oppressors.

The **United Nations,** or **'UN'**, is an international body, a place where all the countries of the world are supposed to come together to prevent war and promote social justice and freedom.

The UDHR sets visionary standards that have helped countless people gain greater freedom and security. It helps prevent human rights abuses and sets clear standards for justice. However, it is often disobeyed and disregarded by governments all over the world. Article 1 famously says, 'We are all born free and equal', yet this is not most people's reality. Human rights are not set in stone. We have to continue to fight for them.

'Surely it is more intelligent to hope rather than to fear, to try rather than not to try. For one thing we know beyond all doubt: nothing has ever been achieved by the person who says "it can't be done."'

Eleanor Roosevelt, 1960, chair of the United Nations Human Rights Commission and a driving force behind the UDHR

Over the years other human rights agreements were established through the UN, focusing on the needs of more marginalised people such as women, refugees and those with disabilities. They are all important for children as well as adults, but they tend to ignore children's particular needs. There was one exception: the 1959 Declaration of the Rights of the Child, which defined basic rights to protection, education, healthcare, shelter and good nutrition.

Core UN human rights treaties

Refugee Convention (1951)

International Convention on the Elimination of all Forms of Racial Discrimination (1966)

International Covenant on Civil and Political Rights (1966)

International Covenant on Economic, Cultural and Social Rights (1966)

Convention on the Elimination of All Forms of Discrimination against Women (1979)

Convention Against Torture and Other Cruel, Inhuman and Degrading Treatment or Punishment (1984)

Convention on the Rights of the Child (1989)

International Convention on the Protection of the Rights of All Migrant Workers and Members of Their Families (1990)

International Convention for the Protection of All Persons from Enforced Disappearances (2006)

Convention on the Rights of Persons with Disabilities (2006)

Africa is the first continent to adopt its own child rights charter, the African Charter on the Rights and Welfare of the Child, 1990. All fifty-four African countries have also ratified the Convention (see below). The African Charter builds on the Convention's principles and highlights issues of special importance in Africa, such as protecting children who are internally displaced, whose guardian is in prison, and who become pregnant while still at school. It has its own committee to which children, or adults acting on their behalf, can bring complaints.

THE UN CONVENTION ON THE RIGHTS OF THE CHILD

'The child should be . . . brought up in the spirit of peace, dignity, tolerance, freedom, equality and solidarity.'

UN Convention on the Rights of the Child, 1989

At last, in 1989, came the Convention on the Rights of the Child. For the first time ever, governments all over the world agreed that the rights of children should have the same recognition as those of adults. They also said that for any society to be strong, its children need to flourish. Under the terms of the Convention, governments are obliged to meet children's basic needs and help every child reach their full potential.

In order to work out how to protect the rights of children, bearing in mind their specific needs, the drafters of the Convention had to address what can place children at risk. It is this: children depend on adults. Dependency brings benefits, but it also has risks. It can make you vulnerable.

In an ideal childhood, you are loved and looked after by adults and all your needs are met. You grow, you thrive, you spread your wings. But this does not always happen. The adults you depend on may not be able to support you. They may be poor, without enough food to give you. They might be ill and unable to look after you properly. Some adults may deliberately abuse you. On top of this, social inequality exists everywhere. You may be discriminated against for many reasons, such as for being a girl, or if you belong to an **Indigenous** group. You may struggle to have enough food and water, because your water source has been poisoned by a chemical company, for example. Your country may be affected by government mismanagement or corruption. You may be living through a war. There

are a whole host of possible scenarios that are not under your control and that can make you vulnerable.

PRECIOUS FREEDOMS

In its entirety, the Convention has 54 **Articles**, each of which applies everywhere, in the home and wider society. They include your rights, a set of rules for governments to uphold them, as well as procedures of the UN Committee on the Rights of the Child. The Committee is a body of eighteen independent child rights experts who regularly monitor how well governments are protecting child rights in their countries.

The Convention looks at childhood in the round, so all of your rights are interlinked and none of them is more important than the others. It makes governments responsible for upholding your rights and for working with other adults to ensure you can enjoy them. Everywhere, parents and guardians have a duty to support all your rights and you have the right to participate in all decisions that affect you. The Convention recognises that as children develop, you have less need for protection because you are increasingly able to take on responsibility. Children in different environments and cultures, with diverse life experiences and capabilities, will mature at different ages. The legal term for this is your **evolving capacities**. It means that you will have increasing autonomy (independence) as you mature.

The Convention is the most ratified human rights treaty in the world, meaning that nearly all governments have signed it and are legally bound to uphold it. This shows that its importance is almost universally accepted. The United States of America is the only country that hasn't ratified it. However, many child rights apply through other US laws and international human rights treaties, so the courts and the government still have to consider the best interests of children. If you live in the United States, you are not unprotected.

Some countries uphold children's rights by embedding the Convention's rules into their own national laws. This is called **direct incorporation**, sometimes known as **domestic incorporation**. It means that child rights are integrated into all legislation that affects children, such as in schools, hospitals and local authorities. It gives you more of a say in how rights are put into practice.

However, other governments have applied what are called **reservations** to certain rights. Reservations can be used as get-out clauses, allowing those governments not to uphold some rights fully.

THE GENERAL PRINCIPLES

Your rights are underpinned by four General Principles. These are fundamental, because the makers of the Convention used them in all their discussions. They also make a very useful lens to help understand your rights.

They are:

- The right to life, survival and development.
- Equality and non-discrimination.
- The right to be heard and to participate.
- The best interests of the child.

The General Principles say very clearly that children are not the passive property of adults. You have a part to play in decision-making, alongside your parents and other adults. You are people with equal dignity and are entitled to respect. Traditionally, people often talk about children in future terms, as if your right to participate in decisions only comes later. '*When you grow up, you can . . .*' The Convention, however, recognises that everyone misses out if the world only pays attention to adults' perspectives. Children and young people have valid, unique and important insights to offer right now.

YOUR RIGHTS ARE EQUAL AND INTERLINKED

No one child right is more important than another. They are all connected. For children and young people to flourish, you need *all* your rights.

Sometimes it's hard to see rights as equal. If you don't have enough food, hunger will be at the forefront of your mind. If you are being physically abused, the pain can feel overwhelming. Being denied an education is immeasurably unfair. The impact of any denial of rights can be long-lasting and its legacy can also affect your own future children, if you become a parent.

It can be tempting to believe that *my* rights are more important than *yours*, especially for anyone in a difficult situation. Desperation can easily cause misdirection of anger. Sometimes called **scapegoating**, this is blaming people who are just as badly off as you, if not worse, rather than holding those in power to account. It often leads to conflict. Tradition and culture can also play a part in how people think about and approach rights.

Knowledge is key. Knowing your rights makes it easier to understand how they connect, what's stopping you from enjoying them, and how to claim them.

Child rights overlap and interlink and all of them are underpinned by the General Principles. The Convention includes 54 rights, or Articles, of which Articles 41 to 54 are about how adults and governments must work together to make sure you can enjoy all your rights.

This book takes Articles 1 to 40 and groups them into core themes. We also look at Article 42 because it says that all governments have an obligation to educate children and adults about child rights.

These are your rights

Life, dignity and health

You have the right to life and an adequate standard of living, including housing, food, water, a clean climate, health and healthcare.

Equality and non-discrimination

You have equal rights with all other children in the world, no matter your race, ethnicity, gender, sexuality, religion, language, parental politics, your own political opinion, wealth, poverty or if you have a disability.

Participation

You have the right to be heard and to participate in all decisions affecting you, including in court. You have the right to receive information.

Identity

You have the right to a name and nationality. This is your legal identity that enables you to access all your other rights.

Safe place

You have the right to a safe place to live and to be cared for, including if you are a refugee, migrant, living on the streets, orphaned, adopted or fostered.

Protection from harm

You have the right not to be tortured or to be treated in a cruel, inhuman or degrading way. You have the right not to be subjected to mental, emotional or physical abuse, dangerous work, forced labour, drugs or sex trafficking.

Bodily integrity

You have the right to be protected from sexual abuse, female genital mutilation (also known as cutting) and early or forced marriage.

Protection from armed violence

You have the right to life and to be protected from war and armed conflict. If you're underage you should not be asked to fight or take part in war.

Criminal justice and liberty

You have the right not to be punished in a cruel, harmful or degrading way. You are entitled to a fair hearing and judges must consider your age and needs. You should receive support to help you recover from abuse.

Privacy

You have the right to privacy and to be protected from bullying, intimidation, harassment, threats and attacks on your reputation.

Minority and Indigenous rights

You have the right to enjoy your own culture, practise your religion and use your languages if you belong to a minority or Indigenous group.

Education

You have the right to information, a good education and schooling to help develop your personality, talents and abilities. You have the right to information and guidance. You have the right to know your rights.

Play

You have the right to play, rest, choose your own friends, share ideas and enjoy the arts and culture.

Freedom of thought

You have the right to your own ideas. You can choose to follow your own faith or none.

Voice and peaceful protest

You have the right to express your views and to join with others to do so, including in peaceful protest. You are entitled to seek out and receive information.

THE OPTIONAL PROTOCOLS

Since the Convention came into being, three optional protocols have been added to provide extra protection and safety measures. Governments choose whether or not they will **ratify** these. If your government hasn't done so, you have the right to campaign to make any of the protocols law in your country.

OPTIONAL PROTOCOL 1 (OP 1) ON THE INVOLVEMENT OF CHILDREN IN ARMED CONFLICT

This aims to strengthen the Convention's existing protections against being recruited to fight in wars and conflict. By 2020, 170 countries out of 197 had ratified OP 1. A further ten countries had signed but not yet ratified, which means they intend to make it binding on them at a time in the future. Seventeen had neither signed nor ratified.

OPTIONAL PROTOCOL 2 (OP 2) ON THE SALE OF CHILDREN, CHILD PROSTITUTION AND CHILD PORNOGRAPHY

This aims to protect you from sexual exploitation and abuse. By 2020, 176 countries had ratified OP 2, nine had signed but not yet ratified, and twelve had taken no action.

OPTIONAL PROTOCOL 3 (OP 3) ON A COMMUNICATIONS PROCEDURE

This came into force in 2014. It allows you, or someone on your behalf, to lodge a complaint with the United Nations Committee on the Rights of the Child about violations of your rights, when your own country's legal system hasn't resolved the issue. Governments that ratify it enshrine the 'right to complain' in law and enable children and young people to have more consistent and reliable access to their rights. OP 3 is essential as the UN does not have an international police force with a remit to enforce child rights, which means that it is up to children, or adults on your behalf, to do this. OP 3 makes it easier because it aids international scrutiny of a government's actions as well as upholding your right to a voice. By 2020, 47 states and countries out of 197 had ratified OP 3.

PART TWO

UNDERSTAND YOUR RIGHTS

'The truth is that we are not yet free; we have merely achieved the freedom to be free, the right not to be oppressed . . . For to be free is not merely to cast off one's chains, but to live in a way that respects and enhances the freedom of others.'

Nelson Mandela, anti-apartheid activist who spent 27 years in prison before becoming President of South Africa, 1994.

2

YOUR RIGHTS IN REALITY

Human rights, including child rights, matter in the real world and they affect you every day.

When you're enjoying your rights you probably aren't aware of them. If you're happy, well-fed, with a home, education and a loving family and friends, your rights are working well for you. But if you're hungry, experiencing violence, without a safe home or an education, and if you're not being heard, this is because your rights are being abused or violated.

This chapter sets out your rights and explores the gaps between them and reality. It includes true accounts of child activists who have fought to make a difference across the world.

LIFE, DIGNITY AND HEALTH

You have the right to life, survival and development, an adequate standard of living and the highest achievable standard of health. Your best interests are paramount. This includes having access to clean drinking water, decent sanitation, adequate housing, enough nutritious food, a clean environment and appropriate healthcare. Every child has the right to benefit from social security. Governments must give parents the help they need to raise you, including financial and other support services. Governments must also ensure you are educated about health, hygiene, nutrition and sanitation so you know how to stay healthy. They should do as much as they can to prevent the deaths of children and young people. Governments have a duty to promote and encourage international cooperation in relation to health.

From Articles 3, 6, 18, 24, 26 and 27

WHAT DOES IT MEAN?

Your right to life, survival and development is integral for you to enjoy your other rights. It is also one of the General Principles (see page 25). The right to health is key. Your physical and mental health and well-being depend on you and your family having access to nutritious food, adequate housing, clean drinking water, decent sanitation and affordable healthcare. For that, you also need a clean climate and a sustainable environment.

You have a better chance of surviving illness and disease if you have good living conditions, food and clean water.

WHAT'S THE REALITY?

One in six children were living in extreme poverty in 2019, a number that rose significantly with the global Covid-19 pandemic. If your family can't afford somewhere safe to live, and you don't know where your next meal is coming from, it presents a huge challenge to your survival and development. Many children and young people go hungry, live in poor housing without basic services such as water and toilets, and grow up without health education. This can be because of lack of resources, but also because of negligence and discrimination. Governments may often favour more privileged groups of people.

Young people often take on adult responsibilities. This is especially true if you live in an area affected by famine, drought or conflict. You may have to work or care for your siblings, forcing you to drop out of school, marry early, or engage in transactional sex just to survive. You are more likely to suffer from malnutrition, injuries, diarrhoeal diseases, unwanted pregnancies, sexual violence, sexually-transmitted diseases and mental health issues.

In the first thirty years since the Convention was adopted, progress on child rights saw the death rate for children under the age of five more than halve. The Convention is working, but there is much more to do. In 2018, about 6.2 million children and young people under the age of fifteen died, mostly from preventable causes. Children under the age of five are still most at risk, mainly because of malnutrition and curable diseases.

Governments have an obligation to uphold your right to health and healthcare, including taking all necessary steps to prevent, control and treat disease. Many of these diseases are spread by lack of basic sanitation, but in 2020 nearly 820 million children still did not have basic handwashing facilities at school, putting them at greater risk of catching and spreading infections.

Health crises such as HIV/AIDS, Ebola and Covid-19 have a huge impact on child rights, beyond the immediate risk to life. In 2016, around the world 120,000 children died due to AIDS-related illnesses. The Ebola epidemic of 2014-16 forced 5 million children out of school for up to nine months in the West African nations of Sierra Leone, Guinea and Liberia. Many never went back. With the onset of the global Covid-19 pandemic in 2020, about a billion children and young people couldn't attend school or university for many months. Many of them were unable to access any learning at this time.

Epidemics and pandemics make it extremely hard for families to make a living. This puts more young people at risk of child labour, sexual exploitation, teenage pregnancy and child marriage. Heightened stress can lead to more domestic violence. Deaths from disease cause large numbers of children to be orphaned and made vulnerable to further exploitation and abuse. Economies struggle to recover from major health crises, with the greatest impact on rights usually being felt by poor and marginalised people.

Health crises and pandemics are thought to be caused or aggravated by human failure to protect biodiversity and the environment. Our increasing encroachment on wildlife may accelerate the emergence and spread of new diseases.

Damage to our environment caused by the **climate crisis** is probably the biggest threat to child rights and ultimately to human survival. Excessive carbon emissions, mainly from wealthier countries, continue to threaten the future of all children. As the planet heats up, it will cause more drought, famine, extreme weather events and diseases such as malaria and dengue, as well as an increase in violence and mental health issues. About a million animal and plant species could likely become extinct.

Some of the world's poorest people live in areas vulnerable to climate change. More than half a billion children live in zones of very high flood occurrence, for example. Drought, famine and floods can force families to leave their homes, and the UN estimates that unchecked climate change could create up to a billion refugees and migrants by 2050. Child refugees and migrants are at increased risk of abuse, neglect, trafficking and child labour and are unlikely to receive an education.

Between 2030 and 2050, climate change is expected to cause approximately 250,000 extra deaths every year, from malnutrition, malaria, diarrhoea and heat stress. Women and children are fourteen times more likely than men to die during a climate-related disaster, such as a major storm. There will also be a huge cost to sectors like agriculture, water and sanitation, which directly affect health. The extra cost is estimated to be between US$2 to 4 billion a year by 2030.

Air pollution also has a serious impact on your right to life and health. Worldwide, 300 million children live in areas with extremely toxic levels of air pollution. About two billion of you live in areas where pollution levels are higher than the minimum air quality standards set by the World Health Organisation. The effects are terrible. Every year, nearly 600,000 children under the age of five die from diseases caused or made worse by the effects of air pollution. Millions more suffer from respiratory diseases.

Your health and development are affected by what you eat and drink. Poverty is a huge factor. Many families are unable to afford the costs of healthy food for children. Your right to health also suffers at the hands of aggressive business marketing tactics. If you are repeatedly exposed to commercial marketing of junk food and sugary drinks, you are more likely to buy them. Globally the number of obese children and teenagers increased from 11 million in 1975 to 124 million in 2016.

> In 2018, almost four million children in the UK lived in households that struggled to afford or access enough fruit, vegetables, fish and other healthy foods to meet the official nutrition guidelines.

FIGHT FOR RIGHTS
TAKING ACTION

'Having access to clean drinking water is a basic human right. Every person, no matter their race, economic status or where they live, needs clean water. Everything needs clean water to survive on this planet.'

Autumn Peltier is also known as 'Water Warrior'. She is an Anishinaabe member of the Wikwemikong First Nation people of Canada. Many Indigenous territories in Canada are subjected to 'boil water advisories', which are warnings that the local water is too contaminated to drink and sometimes should not even be used for washing. Drinking the water without boiling it first can cause nausea, cramps, diarrhoea, and headaches, as well as diseases like cholera, typhoid

fever and dysentery. Canada is one of the wealthiest and most water-rich nations in the world. Its government has strict regulations for water quality and access to safe water is easy for most Canadians. However, First Nations Indigenous communities live on land known as reserves, where the regulations do not apply. Their water is often contaminated, hard to access or has faulty treatment systems.

Autumn was inspired by her great-aunt Josephine Mandamin, who had shown her how to protect the sacred waters on their land. Autumn learned about boil water advisories and that the local water was poisoned.

In Ontario, Canada, there were over sixty-one Indigenous communities who couldn't drink their water – some of whom hadn't been able to do so for over twenty years. As time went by, Autumn noticed her great-aunt's health slowly deteriorating. She worried about who would protect the waters in her place. Just before her great-aunt passed away, she told

Autumn to keep up the work: 'Don't stop loving and protecting the waters, don't let anyone stop you from doing your work, don't stop, keep going.'

> ❙ I thought our country was wealthy and we didn't have third world conditions, but my people live in third world conditions to this very day. I felt that something needed to be done about this, and this is when my journey began. I was eight years old.'

Since then, Autumn spoke at the United Nations World Water Day in 2018, when she was thirteen. She has won awards, including being honoured by the Assembly of First Nations as a water protector. She continues her work for access to clean water for her community and for Indigenous people across the world.

TAKING ACTION

Khairiyah Rahmanyah, also known as 'Daughter of the Sea', was born to a fishing family who live close by the sea in southern Thailand. She grew up by the water, like many children in her district of Chana. The sea outside her home is a rich source of seafood and home to endangered marine species, such as sea turtles and rare pink dolphins.

In 2020, when she was seventeen, she launched a campaign against the Thai government's plan to develop Chana into an industrial estate. She spent many hours picketing, and also travelled 1,000 kilometres to Government House in Bangkok to deliver a letter to the prime minister, begging him to stop the development. She said that the development would disrupt the culture and livelihoods of local people and seriously damage the area's rich marine resources. As a result, the authorities agreed to postpone their decision. However at the time of writing, the verdict still hung in the balance and she continued to campaign.

> I live with the sea, eat from the sea and grew up with the sea. There is a tie between us – a strong one. I want to grow into adulthood in a place filled with environmental wealth just like we have now. I want the next generations to have the right to grow up in the same nature I grew up in.'

TAKING ACTION

In 2018, when Greta Thunberg was fifteen years old, she started protesting in front of the parliament in her home country of Sweden. She demanded that the Swedish government meet the carbon emissions target agreed by world leaders in 2015. She held up a sign that read 'School Strike for Climate' and regularly missed school on Fridays.

Her protests went viral on social media. Support grew and other strikes started around the world, spreading with the hashtag #FridaysForFuture. By December 2018, more than 20,000 students had joined her. She succeeded in changing many people's attitudes and in the process she built a movement for climate action. In September 2019, 4 million people in 161 countries joined the global climate strike – the largest climate demonstration in history.

Greta followed this with an impassioned speech to world leaders at the UN Climate Action Summit:

> You are failing us. But the young people are starting to understand your betrayal. The eyes of all future generations are upon you. And if you choose to fail us, I say: we will never forgive you. We will not let you get away with this. Right here, right now is where we draw the line. The world is waking up. And change is coming, whether you like it or not.'

In the same month, Greta and fifteen other child activists from around the world petitioned the UN Committee on the Rights of the Child, protesting their governments' failure to take action on the climate crisis (see page 242).

TAKING ACTION

> Do all you can with what you have, in the time you have, in the place you are.'

Nkosi Johnson was born in South Africa in 1989. From birth, he had Human Immunodeficiency Virus (HIV), a chronic condition that weakens the immune system and ultimately leads to AIDS. His mother

Nonthlanthla Daphne Nkosi had unknowingly passed the virus on to her unborn child. In those early days of the disease, an effective treatment had not yet been found and great stigma was attached to it.

When Nkosi turned two, he was admitted to hospital. Daphne was terrified to take him back home to the township afterwards, as the intense stigma meant she was likely both to lose her job and their home. She turned to Nkosi's doctor for advice. He was on the board of a home for gay men with AIDS, and he asked its founder, Gail Johnson, if she would take Nkosi in. She and Daphne both agreed. Later, Daphne gave permission for Gail to take Nkosi into her own home and to give him her surname to help with the monthly hospital visits.

Daphne died in 1997. In the same year, Nkosi came to public attention when he wasn't allowed to attend a school in Johannesburg because of his HIV status. He and Gail campaigned for change and were successful.

New anti-discrimination policies were put in place that stopped children being banned from schools based on their health. Nkosi carried on campaigning and together with Gail created Nkosi's Haven, a refuge for mothers and children living with HIV.

In 2000, when he was eleven, Nkosi was invited to be keynote speaker at an International AIDS Conference. At the opening event he said: 'Care for us and accept us, we are all human beings. We are normal. We have hands. We have feet. We can walk, we can talk, we have needs just like everyone else. Don't be afraid of us – we are all the same.' His speech had an enormous impact on public opinion.

When Nkosi died in 2001 he was given a hero's funeral, attended by thousands of mourners, and was posthumously awarded the International Children's Peace Prize.

Since Nkosi's death, scientific advances mean that a pregnant woman with HIV can be treated to prevent the transmission of the disease to the foetus. People with HIV can now expect to live as long as someone without the virus, provided they are on effective treatment and have good access to medical care.

EQUALITY AND NON-DISCRIMINATION

Everyone under the age of majority [usually eighteen, but check your country's rules] has the same rights. You are equal before the law no matter your race, ethnicity or colour, gender, gender identity, language, religion, culture, sexuality, or whether you have a disability, are neurodiverse or rich or poor. If you have a disability you also have rights to special education and care so that you can lead a full life with dignity and as much independence as possible.

From Articles 1, 2 and 23, and Committee on the Rights of the Child General Comment number 13.

WHAT DOES IT MEAN?

Equality is one of the General Principles of the Convention. This says that *all* children deserve the best start possible in life, no matter who you are. No one should suffer because of prejudice and discrimination. Nor should anyone be given extra favours because of who you are or who you know. The Convention also says that children have rights just as adults do – you have equal status as rights holders.

Equality upholds diversity because it's a value that celebrates human differences. As individuals, every child deserves an equal opportunity to flourish and lead a full life. It is humankind's wonderful differences that enrich society. Equality benefits everyone.

Discrimination arises out of prejudice and is one of the main causes of unfair treatment. Discrimination seeks to benefit some people at the expense of others, so it conflicts with equality. It is demeaning for both victim and perpetrator.

WHAT'S THE REALITY?

At the heart of all forms of discrimination are power structures, holding onto privilege and resources. Power structures often feed on concepts of difference or otherness – the myth that one group is better than another – and over time they turn into prejudice.

Discrimination that is arbitrary, or cannot be justified, is against human rights. But it persists. It enables some people to benefit at the expense of others. It creates inequality and injustice, which makes it even harder for people to escape poverty and makes them vulnerable to their rights being abused.

Some governments try to reinforce their power by justifying discrimination in the name of morality, religion or ideology. Discrimination is sometimes cemented in national law, even when it breaks international law. States sometimes try to build power structures based on the idea that certain groups are less important and more likely to be criminal, simply for who they are, such as being poor, Indigenous or Black.

There are many forms of discrimination. Here are a few. All of them are contrary to the Convention as well as other international human rights treaties.

Racism

Racism is discrimination fuelled by an ideology that has affected every country in the world for centuries. It is based on the false principle that you can divide people by 'race' and that people with white skin are superior and should dominate those with brown or black skin. It systematically denies people their full human rights because of their colour, **ethnicity** (cultural heritage, as opposed to skin colour), descent (including **caste**) or national origin.

Science shows there is no such thing as distinct biological races, but many people still believe in the concept and use it to justify hatred, persecution and murder. This is racism, pure and simple. Racism and **white supremacy** – entrenched views that white people are better – cause the oppression of Black people and **people of colour** on a daily basis. Businesses and individuals who spread these views can make a lot of money through perpetuating fear.

Race doesn't exist on a biological level, only on a social one. In other words, it's what society has conditioned us to think for centuries, rather than being based on fact. Over the past few decades, scientific research has proven that all humans are extremely closely related. We all have the same collection of genes. We all originate from Africa.

Between 1525 and 1866, European and American traders profited from the enslavement of at least 12 million African people in the transatlantic slave trade, using racism to justify their cruel, inhuman and degrading treatment. Racism causes great pain and suffering. If it is left unchecked, it fuels atrocities and genocides.

Gender discrimination

In many countries, all over the world, there are laws, policies, customs and beliefs that deny rights to girls. Many governments openly support measures that repress girls and women. For example, if you are a girl in Saudi Arabia, you face lifelong discrimination. Even as an adult, you will be treated like a small child under the male guardianship system, whereby a man (usually your father or husband, but it could be your brother or son) has the power to control your life from your birth until your death. The system does not allow you to make any critical decisions by yourself. Women were not allowed to drive cars until 2018, and girls and women cannot apply for a passport or travel without the permission of a male guardian.

In all countries, there are persistent attitudes that encourage boys and men to dominate. These attitudes are known as gender stereotyping, and can limit your choices, your aspirations and your life. It causes discrimination and a long chain of human rights violations. In 2019 the United Nations Children's Fund (UNICEF) found that a quarter of girls worldwide between the ages of fifteen and nineteen are not in education, paid work or training, compared with one tenth of boys. If you are denied an education due to your gender, you are more likely to face pressure to marry early, to have children at a young age and be unable to work. It makes it very hard to achieve your potential. Gender-based violence causes great suffering across the world (see Bodily integrity, page 92).

Homophobia and transphobia

Everywhere in the world, people face discrimination because of who they love, who they are attracted to and who they are. Lesbian, gay, bisexual, transgender and intersex (LGBTI) people risk being unfairly treated in all areas of their lives. They often face harassment and violence.

Consensual same-sex sexual activity – agreed to and freely entered into by both partners – is illegal in some seventy-eight countries. Being gay or lesbian could see you sentenced to death in Iran, Saudi Arabia, Yemen, Mauritania, Sudan, as well as some regional areas in Nigeria and Somalia.

So-called 'gay conversion therapy' claims to be based on science but is completely bogus. It tries to remove feelings of same-sex attraction or to force someone to identify with their recorded birth gender. According to the UN, young people are disproportionately affected. Yet conversion therapy is unscientific, not medically certified and is deeply degrading and harmful. By 2020, five countries (Brazil, Ecuador, Germany, Malta

and Taiwan) and 20 US states had banned its use on children, with others likely to follow suit.

Children and young people with gender dysphoria face the added burden of having to prove who they are without legal documentation (such as a passport) that recognises their self-identified gender. Some countries, such as Nepal and New Zealand, are now beginning to issue gender-neutral documentation.

In 2013, Russia passed what is commonly known as the 'gay propaganda law'. This bans young people's access to information about LGBTI people's lives and fosters discrimination. It has been used to shut down online information and mental health referral services for children, as well as to discourage support groups and mental health professionals from working with young LGBTI people. It has contributed to a rise in violence and harassment against LGBTI children and adults.

On the other side of the world, Chile's Amaranta School opened in 2018. It is believed to be the world's first school created for transgender students, their siblings and any other child who has found it difficult to fit into traditional schools. It was set up to give a safe and welcoming space to young people who have been bullied for who they are.

A trans, or transgender, person is anybody whose gender identity differs from what is typically associated with the sex they were assigned at birth. It's also an umbrella term that covers a range of gender identities. **Gender dysphoria** refers to the emotional distress caused by the conflict between someone's apparent gender and the gender with which they identify. **Non-binary gender** is used to describe people who do not experience themselves as either male or female (in other words, they aren't within the gender binary). They fall within the wider definition of transgender because they have not remained in the gender they were assigned at birth.

Transgenderism is not a modern concept. To take just one example, the transgendered *hijras* of India are part of a tradition that goes back at least 2,000 years.

Disability discrimination

About one in ten children have a physical or mental disability, and 80% of people with disabilities (both adults and children) live in developing countries.

If you have a disability, of course you have exactly the same rights as all children and young people. However, you probably face extra challenges in accessing those rights. You are disabled by barriers in society, not your impairment or difference. Discrimination can mean that other people don't adapt to your needs. Unnecessary obstacles are often placed in your way and many opportunities are unfairly denied to you, even going to school. Buildings and other public facilities are often inaccessible and are created without you in mind. Your government may set policies (rules that guide a country's systems, such as welfare or transport) that exclude you. Girls with disabilities are also two to three times more likely to face physical and sexual abuse than girls without disabilities.

Poverty, class and caste

Every country has people living in extreme poverty, on the margins of society, without shelter, income or enough food. In 2013, about 385 million children lived in extreme poverty. Children in these conditions also struggle to access education and are more likely to be discriminated against. It makes it harder to have a fair start in life, or an equal opportunity to thrive. If you also live in a war-affected area or one that is vulnerable to climate-related disasters, extra obstacles are placed in your way. None of this means it is impossible to succeed, but it shows that the odds against you are higher, despite governments' obligations to uphold your rights.

In developing countries, children in the poorest 20% of the population are up to three times more likely to die before their fifth birthday than children in the richest 20%.

FIGHT FOR RIGHTS
TAKING ACTION

' Asking me to change my hair is like asking me to erase my blackness.'

In 2016, when she was thirteen, Zulaikha Patel and other Black school students marched against Pretoria High School for its racist and sexist hair policy. The school had instructed students to 'fix' or chemically straighten their hair and had enforced its rules using racially derogatory language. South Africa is a country where apartheid laws had ruled every aspect of life on racial lines from 1948 until the 1990s, so the hair policy wasn't an oversight. The school also prohibited African languages and did not allow Black girls to gather in groups of more than four. The protest highlighted how deeply racist discrimination still runs in South Africa. Zulaikha and other protesters at her school refused to comply with private security guards who had been hired to disperse the demonstration and who were armed with AK-47 rifles and dogs. The guards threatened to arrest the students, leading to a collective standoff.

The girls used social media to communicate their cause. The hashtag #StopRacismAtPretoriaGirlsHigh was used over 150,000 times and brought together Black students in a collective sharing of grievances about former white institutions. The protest inspired similar actions at other schools. A government minister visited. The US ambassador to South Africa tweeted: 'All societies have rules. And sometimes those rules are biased and need to be exposed and protested.' An online petition raised almost 25,000 signatures in a day. It worked. The regional department of education suspended the hair policy.

Apartheid was a system of institutionalised racial segregation in South Africa that lasted from 1948 until the early 1990s. It gave power to the country's minority white population.

TAKING ACTION

'If you are ignorant of your rights, you can easily be taken advantage of by evil-minded people. If you know your rights, you will not be cheated easily.'

Aisha Saleh lives with her brother and grandmother in a slum area of Lagos, the biggest city in Nigeria. She speaks five languages and has been an activist since she was eleven, fighting for the right to education and against child marriage, in collaboration with the Nigerian child rights organisation CEE-HOPE.

In 2019 she won a place to represent Nigeria at the United Nations International Children's Conference in Geneva, Switzerland, but the Nigerian passport office blocked her, refusing to believe her travel plans because she was poor.

A year later, when she was fifteen, Aisha began a

campaign on **period poverty** and tackled the cultural taboo on talking about menstruation. She urged the Nigerian government to provide free menstrual products to girls like her, who cannot afford sanitary products so miss school when they are menstruating. She highlighted the reality: that poverty and government negligence make girls from poor backgrounds more vulnerable. Some girls offer sex in exchange for money to buy menstrual products; others are forced into early marriage. Aisha's campaign succeeded in raising awareness and normalising discussion of the topic. Many people donated money and pads for distribution to girls across Nigeria, including in camps for displaced people. Aisha continued to push politicians for free distribution of sanitary pads to girls and women, especially in poor and vulnerable communities and schools.

TAKING ACTION

In Colombia, two teenage students, Pablo Enrique Torres Gutiérrez and José Prieto Restrepo, took their church-run school to court for excluding them for being gay. The case was referred to the Colombian Supreme Court. In 1998 the boys won their case. Since then, the country has developed a significantly inclusive legal framework to protect LGBTI rights.

However, in practice these rights are not greatly upheld. There is ongoing discrimination. In 2019, out of nine countries in Latin America and the Caribbean, Colombia registered the highest number of killings of LGBTI people over a five-year period.

TAKING ACTION

Emily Waldron is a twelve-year-old British transgender girl. She had always thought she was the only person like her until she went to a meeting run by a charity called Mermaids, which supports young transgender people and their families. After this,  Emily decided to do whatever she could to make sure that no one else in her position felt isolated. She attended a meeting at Amnesty International, where she talked to civil servants from the British government's equalities office about the Gender Recognition Act, which allows some trans people to change their legal gender on birth certificates. It made her realise there are many ways to campaign for rights and equality. Since then she has taken part in various campaigns.

Emily says:

> Campaigning makes me feel powerful and in control of my destiny. When I started secondary school, I started an LGBT and allies club. I gave speeches at each year group assembly to inform my peers and they were really popular. I want all pupils to feel safe and part of the school community. I will keep campaigning until I get the love, equality and respect that my community and I deserve, because we are all human and we should all be one big community and support each other.'

TAKING ACTION

In Wales, Amy, Jaime, Kane and Jamie were aged between eleven and fourteen when they began to fight discrimination in 2019. The girls have additional learning needs and the boys are wheelchair users. They faced frequent verbal abuse and found it hard to move around because of many obstacles in the way, such as cars parked on pavements. So they applied to the police for **hate crime** funding and used the money to buy

video cameras. Then they documented the evidence. They put together a powerful evidence report with the video, pointing to their rights under the Convention to support their demands for change. The video was launched at the Welsh Parliament. They also presented it to regional councillors and decision makers, who pledged their support and made an action plan for change. In their report they said:

> We just want the same rights as everyone else in our communities.'

TAKING ACTION

Ukei Muratalieva is a disability rights activist and well-known fashion designer in Kyrgyzstan. When she was a small child, she wasn't allowed to go to nursery because the staff said it was not adapted for children with disabilities and not safe for her.

I was born with cerebral palsy and some of my earliest memories are of being kept under lock and key at home. My dad died when I was very little and Mum had to provide for my brothers and me on her own. So every morning my brothers went to school and Mum went to work, leaving me at home on my own. For most of my childhood I felt lonely and excluded.'

For Ukei to be allowed to go school, her mother had to sign a document saying that the school bore no responsibility for any accidents. Only one teacher agreed to have Ukei in her class.

She faced more battles – such as state exams not being adapted for people with disabilities – but eventually she studied fashion design at university and embarked on a successful career.

She and other campaigners achieved a major breakthrough in 2019, when the UN Convention on the Rights of Persons with Disabilities was ratified by the Kyrgyzstan government. Today she is the board chair of the non-governmental organisation Nazik Kyz, promoting the rights of girls and women with disabilities.

PARTICIPATION

You have the right to be heard and to participate in all decisions affecting you, including in courts. You have the right to receive information.

From Article 12

WHAT DOES IT MEAN?

This is a pillar of the Convention, rooted in the General Principles (see page 25).

Your right to be heard and to participate means that you should be listened to and taken seriously on all decisions that affect you. When you participate, you develop as an individual, but it's more than this. Your perspective on an issue or a problem helps everyone reach better decisions, so society is strengthened too. Participation rights are closely linked to your evolving capacities (see page 23) and apply in whatever way is most appropriate for you. Young children's participation, for example, will be mainly limited to issues in the family and close environment. But as you mature and develop, you can involve yourself in a whole host of issues, from local to national to international.

At school, you should have a say in your own education and how your school is run. If you are in care, you should be involved whenever a decision is being made about you. If you have to go to hospital, the doctors and nurses should give you information, listen to you and take you seriously.

For any court or legal proceedings, the Committee on the Rights of the Child says that the adults involved should presume you are capable of forming your own view and that you shouldn't have to prove yourself. It also says that younger children are capable of forming their own views even if they are not capable of expressing them verbally. For this reason, courts are encouraged to consider non-verbal forms of communication (such as facial expressions, play and drawing) so a young child can express their understanding and preferences in their own way.

Governments are also legally bound to inform everyone about the provisions of the Convention, by a variety of methods. This should mean that you and the courts know you are entitled to communicate your views. If you are in a situation where this isn't happening, you have the right to inform or remind the court of its legal obligations.

WHAT'S THE REALITY?

Your right to be heard is important to achieve change. It can be challenging, though, as it requires others to listen to you and be open to your ideas in a world that doesn't always regard children as equal to adults. People may belittle you. And if you happen to belong to a minority group, are a girl or have a disability, you may face additional barriers in being heard. However, when children and young people speak up, participate and are taken seriously, it benefits everyone. You can succeed.

> All budgets, regional or national, have significant implications for children and young people. Some authorities encourage children to join the budget planning process. In the municipal assembly of Fortaleza in northern Brazil, for example, children participated in local and national budgetary planning for several years. In 2003, they proposed thirty-three amendments to the municipal budget, three of which were approved for the 2004 budget.

Some governments undertake 'child rights impact assessments'. These are powerful tools that predict the impact of any proposed law, policy or budget allocation on children. They serve your best interests and give you a voice in adult-dominated processes.

They prevent potential harm and minimise the risk of costly mistakes. They can be built into government at all levels and as early as possible in the development of new policies and laws.

> India has set up a national Children's Parliament that is a federation of neighbourhood children's parliaments. Children and young people address local, state, national and international forums about matters that affect their own lives and those of their peers. It is run for and by children.

FIGHT FOR RIGHTS
TAKING ACTION

> Social action has taught me how to speak out in a way that makes people listen. I used to sit quietly in meetings; now I stand up and am heard at a local and national level.'

Charlotte Donaldson is a Scottish Gypsy Traveller who fights for equality, including advising the Scottish government on how to stamp out discrimination against minority groups.

When she was sixteen, she was a founder member of the Scottish Gypsy Traveller Assembly, meeting with representatives of the Scottish Government. She contributed to the Scottish Human Rights Commission report in 2019 and has worked with regional museums to identify and celebrate Gypsy Traveller artefacts. She pushed for their representation at national level on the Scottish Youth Parliament. In 2020 Charlotte and her older brother Davie won a Young Scot Award for their anti-racism advocacy and campaigning work.

She says:

> There is still a long way to go before Gypsies and Travellers have equal rights in this country and I am determined to play a role in tackling stigma and getting more support and protections for my community.'

IDENTITY

Every child has the right to be registered
immediately after birth and to have a name
and nationality. This should be preserved
and protected from unlawful change.

From Articles 7 and 8

WHAT DOES IT MEAN?

This right opens the doors to many other rights, such as
education, health, freedom of movement and political
participation. Being registered after birth gives you a
legal identity. Of course, you still have all the rights
in the Convention regardless, simply because you are
human. However, legal identity is a proof of your
existence. With this proof, the government of your
country of birth formally recognises your identity and
commits to uphold your rights from day one. It means
that society includes you, rather than excludes you.

WHAT'S THE REALITY?

If you're not registered you have no proof of existence.
It makes it nearly impossible to have a nationality. This
means that you may be what is called 'stateless', as
no government will accept you are one of its citizens.

You are invisible in the eyes of the law, making it very difficult to claim your rights. You will struggle to do all the activities in everyday life that require proof of identity, such as going to school, enrolling in university, getting a passport or bank account, travelling abroad, receiving care from a doctor, claiming benefits, getting a driver's licence or owning a car. You may never be able to vote and could find it very difficult to work or marry.

> There are an estimated 120,000 children in the UK who do not have British citizenship or legal permission to live there. More than half of them were born in the UK and many are entitled to register as British citizens under the British Nationality Act 1981. But the registration fee is so high that many cannot afford to pay it. This means they cannot access their other rights and their best interests are ignored.

If you're invisible, you are at greater risk. In practice, you may find countries or states provide you with less protection against trafficking, slavery and other forms of **forced labour** or child prostitution. Instead of the state supporting you, you will more likely have to rely on yourself, your family (if you have one) and the kindness of others – but this isn't safe, it isn't fair and often it's sadly not enough.

It is hard to get exact figures because the nature of the problem means there is no reliable data. But it's estimated there are 290 million unregistered children, living in all regions of the world and most countries. Nearly half (45%) of children aged five and under have not been registered.

The problem doesn't disappear when you grow up. Including adults, about one billion people around the globe face challenges in proving who they are and therefore have trouble in accessing basic services. If you're a girl in a low income country, you only have a 50/50 chance of ever having a legal identity.

It is a United Nations Sustainable Development Goal that by 2030 everyone is able to get a legal identity, including birth registration. But it is unjust that your access to rights and services depends on this.

The UN's global **Sustainable Development Goals (SDGs)** are a plan to achieve a better and more sustainable future for everyone by 2030. They address global challenges including poverty, inequality, climate change, environmental degradation, peace and justice.

There is a whole host of possible reasons why you might not be registered at birth. Most governments don't explain the importance of registration, so many parents simply don't know that it's crucial for their child's future. High fees can make it unaffordable. Poorly equipped registry offices make the process difficult. Others may see your gender or ethnicity as a reason to treat you as less important. Parents who are immigrants may be fearful of how the authorities may treat them, or you may be one of many refugee children who are stateless because you have had to flee your country without legal identity documents. You may have been born in a refugee camp, where it is very hard to gain a nationality. Or you might be part of an undocumented migrant family.

Twenty-seven countries have laws that do not let women pass on their nationality to their children. Some countries won't allow citizenship for people of particular ethnicities.

After over three decades of a 'one-child' policy to limit population size, in 2016 China loosened the rules. But there are high fees to register a second or subsequent child, which many families cannot afford. This has resulted in about 13 million 'invisible children'. Parents hide them because they're afraid they'll be punished for not paying the fees.

FIGHT FOR RIGHTS
TAKING ACTION

Francia Simon's parents fled poverty and violence in Haiti long before she was born and, along with many other refugees, they went to live in the neighbouring Dominican Republic. The village where she grew up is very poor and her family, like many others coming from Haiti, has no official status.

Francia didn't have a birth certificate, so when it was time for her to go to secondary school, she found she couldn't enrol. Her father was partly Dominican, but he had left her and her Haitian mother when she was nine, so neither of her parents could help with registration. Fortunately she had a Dominican aunt who was able to register her, after which she received her birth certificate and could continue her education.

Since then, Francia has fought to improve the situation for others, going from door to door to tell people about their rights. She has helped 900 children to get their birth certificates and access education by guiding them through the complex application process and taking them to the registry office.

'Because of my age and small stature, they thought they could just send me away, a chiquita [little girl] like me. But I wasn't intimidated, I put on a serious, almost angry face, and asked for an appointment.'

In 2010, when Francia was sixteen, she won the International Children's Peace Prize for her work.

SAFE PLACE

You should not be separated from your parents against your will unless it is in your best interests. Every child has the right to special care and protection if you cannot be looked after by your family. Governments must provide safe alternative care for children unable to live with their birth family. They must ensure children are well looked after, in an adoptive or foster home that respects their culture, language and religion, and that conditions are regularly reviewed. The same rules apply to child refugees, children living on the streets and those who are trafficked or abducted and taken abroad. If you are separated from your parents, governments must help you to be reunited.

From Articles 9, 10, 11, 20, 21, 22, 25 and 35

WHAT DOES IT MEAN?

All children have the right to a home where their needs are met, because it gives you a healthy childhood and better life chances. A safe and stable home helps you access your other rights, including health and education. If you are homeless, or you live in slum conditions, in a refugee camp, on the streets or in an institutional setting, you can be more vulnerable to harm and abuse. It makes it very difficult for you to enjoy all your rights and to grow and develop as you should.

'Homeless', 'refugee', 'migrant' or 'living in care' are temporary and incomplete labels. They do not reflect who you are – your story, your personality, your skills or knowledge.

WHAT'S THE REALITY?
Refugees and migrants

Discrimination against migrants and refugees is often based on racism or **xenophobia**. It can be fuelled by some politicians deliberately looking for scapegoats to blame for social or economic problems. Words of hate, frequently repeated and shared across social or mainstream media, can in some cases lead to abuse and even violence.

Refugees are people who are forced to flee their homes, usually because of war, conflict or persecution. However, some families and entire communities have begun to suffer from disasters due to climate change, such as catastrophic flooding, which forces them to leave their homes. It's impossible to return, at least in the short term, because the situation in their country of origin is too dangerous. If this happens to you, you have a universal human right to seek asylum in another country. Globally there were at least 10 million child refugees in 2020.

If you are an **internally displaced** person, you have probably been forced out of your own home by violence and conflict, but you are still in your own country. In 2019 there were at least 17 million internally displaced children around the world.

Many people mistakenly think that, unlike refugees, **migrants** leave home out of 'choice' and can always return. But the reality is that many embark on dangerous journeys because survival at home seems hopeless. Reasons can include extreme poverty and starvation, lack of access to healthcare, lack of education or jobs, environmental crises, high levels of crime, gang-related violence, extortion, kidnap and forced recruitment into armed groups. Girls may be escaping high levels of domestic violence, sexual abuse and rape.

If you are a child refugee or migrant who has become separated from your family, you are especially vulnerable to trafficking or other harm, so you have the right to extra protection.

Children living in street situations

Many millions of children have to live or work on the streets just to survive. Each will have their own reasons, which may include poverty, a broken relationship with parents or carers, physical or sexual abuse, mental health issues or substance abuse. You may be forced to take care of yourself and bear many of the responsibilities of adulthood. Being on the streets makes you more vulnerable to many forms of violence, exploitation and abuse.

Children living in care

You should only be placed in alternative foster or residential care when it is essential for your well-being and safety. There are likely to be complex reasons why your parents cannot look after you, including poor mental health, substance abuse and addictions, neglect, physical abuse and a lack of government support.

It is estimated that at least 2.7 million children live in residential care, but not all countries keep accurate records so the true number is likely to be far higher.

FIGHT FOR RIGHTS
TAKING ACTION

The Glasgow Girls were a group of girls who famously campaigned and changed the law to prevent their school friend from being deported. In 2005, fifteen-year-old Agnesa Murselaj and her mother, both Kosovan Roma refugees in the city of Glasgow, were seized in a dawn raid on their home. They were held in detention and told they would be deported.

Six of Agnesa's friends at Drumchapel High School were outraged and organised a petition to stop proceedings. This grew into a full-blown campaign to end dawn raids and the incarceration of minors, which the girls took to the Scottish Parliament. They won huge support along the way and received the Scottish Campaign of the Year award.

They succeeded in halting Agnesa's expulsion. Five years later their victory was complete when the UK national government put an end to impromptu raids and the detention of children in remand centres.

TAKING ACTION

Balaknama means 'children's voice'. It is an Indian newspaper, formed in 2002, that is written, edited and distributed by children and young people with experience of living on the streets. Their average age is fourteen. Every new reporter who joins is trained by the more experienced ones. Their goal is to change people's perceptions of children living in street situations. In doing this, they are claiming their rights to identity, dignity and a voice. The eight-page tabloid delves into issues faced by children on the streets, including sexual abuse, child labour and police brutality, as well as stories of hope and positive change.

One of Balaknama's achievements was a news report drawing attention to the fact that street-connected children were being forced to retrieve dead bodies from railway tracks. It triggered a public outcry and led to the National Commission for Protection of Child Rights taking disciplinary action against the police.

PROTECTION FROM HARM

You have the right to be protected from torture, cruel, inhuman and degrading treatment, mental, emotional or physical abuse, dangerous work, forced labour, drug abuse and other forms of exploitation. Governments must protect you from being abducted, sold or trafficked. You have the right to support to help you recover from any such abuse.

From Articles 19, 32, 33, 35, 36 and 37

WHAT DOES IT MEAN?

These rights protect you from being hurt and exploited by others. They mean that torture, forced labour and child slavery can never be justified. No one has the right to own, sell, exploit or torture another person.

WHAT'S THE REALITY?

Torture

Torture is when somebody in power inflicts severe mental or physical pain or suffering on somebody else for a specific purpose. Governments commit acts of torture all over the world. Some authorities torture a person to extract a confession or get information, even though it's illegal and notoriously unreliable. Torture is also used as a punishment to spread fear among others. Governments are complicit if they fail to investigate torture allegations or even actively encourage it.

Even if it doesn't amount to torture, it may amount to cruel, degrading and inhuman treatment or punishment. This is also banned in all circumstances. Depriving you of the rights you need to survive – shelter, health, a decent standard of living – could amount to cruel, degrading and inhuman treatment if your situation is dire.

Child labour

There are many kinds of work that involve children and young people. Experiencing the world of work can be good for you, provided it doesn't interfere with your rights to education, play and development. Sometimes you also need to help out with your family's income. But you should never be exploited through long hours without breaks, or dangerous and harmful work and working conditions.

About 152 million children between the ages of five and seventeen are engaged in child labour. About a third don't go to school so are denied an education. Some work might be dangerous (exposing you to toxic chemicals, for example). The highest numbers of child labourers are found in Africa (72.1 million), Asia and the Pacific (62 million), the Americas (10.7 million), Europe and Central Asia (5.5 million) and the Arab States (1.2 million). Many work more than forty-three hours a week. Discrimination based on race, gender, religion and class or caste is likely to worsen the exploitation.

Some of the world's largest companies sell food, cosmetics and other staples that contain palm oil from Indonesia. The palm oil plantations have involved child labourers as young as eight years old. They have been made to work in hazardous conditions and without safety equipment on land where toxic pesticides have been used. This is tough, grinding work that can cause real damage to health and schooling.

In 2016, one boy who dropped out of school to help his father told Amnesty that he had been getting up at 6.00 a.m. for two years, since he was eight. He had to gather and carry palm fruit, six hours a day, six days a week. After Amnesty spoke out, the company in question said that it was taking steps to protect children's rights and prevent child labour.

Thousands of children are used to mine cobalt in the Democratic Republic of the Congo. The cobalt is used to power mobile phones, laptop computers, and other portable electronic devices. Using basic hand tools, miners dig out rocks from tunnels deep underground. Accidents are common. Cobalt is toxic, and if you are exposed to it for a long time it can be fatal, but there is usually no protective equipment. Arthur, who worked in a mine from age nine to eleven, explained: 'I worked in the mines because my parents couldn't afford to pay for food and clothes for me. Papa is unemployed, and Mama sells charcoal.'

Forced labour and slavery

Forced labour is work performed against your will and under the threat of punishment or another penalty, from which you can't easily escape. There are about 5.5 million children engaged in forced labour worldwide. It happens in all countries, especially in construction, agriculture, fisheries, domestic work, mining and sex work. Many children are targeted to make and distribute illegal drugs. Children are often forced into work because their families owe others money which may take years to pay off, if at all. This is called **debt bondage**. Forced labour is one form of child slavery. Debt bondage is another.

Child slavery includes sexual exploitation, forced marriage, domestic slavery such as cleaning, cooking and childcare, forced labour in factories or agriculture, or forced criminal activity, like begging, theft, working on cannabis farms or delivering illegal drugs. (See Bodily integrity, page 92.) There are about 10 million child slaves around the world.

Child **trafficking** is how child slaves are transported, often within the same country. Children make up a third of all victims of trafficking, both for labour and sexual exploitation. Boys are just as likely to be trafficked as girls. Children without a legal identity or fixed home are most vulnerable, but it can happen to anyone. Traffickers are often people you know, like friends or family members. It's big business: between them traffickers make US$150 billion per year. This massive abuse of many child rights has a lifelong impact on survivors' mental and physical health.

The US Department of Labor has developed the Sweat & Toil app, which documents child and forced labour worldwide. Users can find child labour data and identify goods produced with child or forced labour. This knowledge enables them to buy more ethically. It also helps to lower demand for goods made through exploitation.

FIGHT FOR RIGHTS
TAKING ACTION

Iqbal Masih was a Pakistani boy who became what is called a 'debt slave' when he was only about five years old. His family took a loan from a carpet factory owner and Iqbal had to pay it back through working long hours in terrible conditions. He was often beaten.

He escaped when he was ten and attended the Bonded Labour Liberation Front (BLLF) School for former child slaves. As his understanding of human rights grew, he became an outspoken public advocate against child exploitation. Despite the danger, he would slip into factories and talk to children about their experiences. The BLLF sent him to speak at businesses and events all over Pakistan, where he encouraged slave labourers to escape. His public profile grew and he received many death threats from the organised business mafias that dominated the communities. Iqbal then began visiting other countries to raise awareness of child slaves and call for their freedom. In 1994 he received a human rights award.

Tragically, Iqbal was murdered in 1995, when he was just twelve. His killers were never brought to justice.

After his death he was awarded the World Children's Prize. He left a powerful legacy, including the annual Iqbal Masih Award for the Elimination of Child Labor, set up in 2009 by the United States Congress.

TAKING ACTION

In Nigeria, sixteen-year-old Moses Akatugba was waiting for the results of his secondary school exams when he was arrested by the Nigerian army in 2005, shot in the hand and beaten. They suspected him of stealing three mobile phones in an armed robbery nearby, a charge that he denied. He was severely tortured and forced to sign an untrue confession.

After eight years in prison he was sentenced to death by hanging. This was illegal, both because he was a child at the time of the alleged offence and because 'confessions' extracted under torture should not be allowed as evidence in court.

During his time behind bars Moses coached the prison football team to try and keep everyone's hope alive. While on Death Row, he received 800,000 solidarity letters and cards from all over the world after being featured in Amnesty's Write for Rights campaign. Activists including many young people demonstrated outside their country's Nigerian embassies on his behalf. They also called on the Nigerian government to commute the death sentence and hold a public inquiry into the torture.

The pressure worked. Moses was freed in 2019.

> I am overwhelmed. I thank Amnesty International and their activists for the great support that made me a conqueror in this situation. They are my heroes. I want to assure them that this great effort they have shown to me will not be in vain. I promise to be a human rights activist – to fight for others.'

BODILY INTEGRITY

You have the right to be protected from sexual abuse and trafficking, female genital mutilation (cutting) and early forced marriage. You have the right to support to help you recover. You have the right to make informed decisions about your body, health and life.

From Articles 11, 19, 34, 37, 39 and OP 2

WHAT DOES IT MEAN?

Your body is yours to enjoy. No one has the right to do anything to it without your consent. You have the right to be protected from all forms of sexual violence, including rape, female genital mutilation (cutting), forced pregnancy, forced abortion and forced sterilisation. Most of these abuses arise from and perpetuate gender inequality. They are all forbidden.

You also have sexual and reproductive rights. You have the right to get accurate information about your body, your sexual health and relationships so that you can make informed decisions. Depending on the minimum age of sexual consent in your state or country, you are entitled to sexual **agency**. This includes your right to consent to, or decline, intercourse and for your decision to be honoured. Your sexual orientation is for you to determine, not others. You should be able to access health services including contraception, testing and treatment for sexually transmitted infections, including HIV. You have the right to make these choices without fear, violence or discrimination.

Article 39 says you have the right to recover from rights abuses. This means you also have the right to be given support to help you recover.

The age of sexual consent varies around the world. Most countries prohibit sex with under-sixteens or under-eighteens. Nigeria has probably the lowest age of consent in the world, at eleven, but this varies and in some Nigerian states it is eighteen. Laws in different countries can also vary depending on your gender and sexuality.

WHAT'S THE REALITY?

In some countries, young people under the age of sexual consent face stern penalties. Jordan's penal code, for example, criminalises anyone who has sexual intercourse under the age of eighteen. Girls aged twelve to eighteen who are accused of having sex outside marriage may be imprisoned in so-called 'rehabilitation centres'. One of these is Al-Khanza juvenile facility, and many girls sent there are survivors of rape or sexual assault. If they are pregnant, they struggle to safely access an abortion and are also likely to have the child forcibly taken from them. Girls are also subjected to humiliating so-called 'virginity tests' in violation of international law.

Protection from sexual violence

The World Health Organisation estimates that 150 million girls and 73 million boys are sexually assaulted every year. About 10 million children are sexually exploited around the world. Nearly all are afraid of speaking out because of stigma and humiliation. Many worry they will be blamed. Criminals make big profits from trafficking children into sexual slavery.

Girls suffer disproportionately. Globally, more than 14 million teenage girls give birth every year, often because of rape and unwanted pregnancy. Between 2014 and 2017, the armed group calling itself the Islamic State (IS) committed war crimes and **crimes against humanity** against the Yezidi religious minority community in Iraq. IS abducted and enslaved Yezidi children, tortured them, raped them and forced them to fight. Many girls over the age of nine gave birth as a result of rape. For those who survived and returned home, cultural and religious taboos in their own community forced them to give up their children, causing severe anguish.

In many countries, girls who are pregnant often experience intense stigma and discrimination. Many are forced into marriage or to leave school. All girls should have access to medical care and safe abortion services, but in practice there are many legal and practical barriers. The perceived shame of adolescent pregnancy means that many girls undergo unsafe procedures carried out by untrained people in a non-medical environment. They carry great risk.

Pregnancy complications are the top cause of death among fifteen to nineteen-year-old girls worldwide.

In 2015 the Sierra Leone government banned pregnant girls from attending school and sitting exams. This was not just a violation of their right to education, but also reinforced negative gender stereotypes. The ban was enforced through humiliating searches and physical examinations, in violation of girls' rights to physical integrity and privacy. After nearly five years of campaigning, the ban was lifted in December 2019.

There are twenty-six countries where abortion is illegal, even if the pregnancy is the result of incest or rape. In thirty-nine countries, abortion is illegal unless it saves the life of the mother. In 2010, a ten-year-old Paraguayan girl who had been raped by her stepfather was forced to carry on with the pregnancy and give birth, despite the serious risks to her own physical and mental health.

FGM

Female Genital Mutilation (FGM), also known as cutting, is a violent procedure performed on girls. The female genitals are partly or entirely removed or damaged. The purpose is to inhibit a woman's sexual feelings and remove sexual pleasure. Most often the mutilation is performed before puberty, often on girls between the age of four and eight, but sometimes it is done to babies. FGM is dangerous and can result in infection, severe bleeding and death. It is also linked to infertility, pregnancy and childbirth complications in later life. FGM still happens, mainly in North-Eastern, Eastern and Western Africa but also in the Middle East, in South-East Asia and Europe. The World Health Organisation (WHO) estimates that 200 million women are affected by FGM worldwide. It is totally prohibited under the Convention.

By contrast, male circumcision is usually a minor

procedure that carries little risk, involving the removal of a boy's foreskin from his penis. Sometimes it is carried out for medical reasons, but often it is part of religious and cultural tradition. Some people question its validity unless it is on medical grounds.

> In Burkina Faso FGM is carried out on 75% of girls. In Sierra Leone it is even higher: 88%. In Burkina Faso, Senegal and Sierra Leone, between 30% and 50% of girls are forced to marry before they turn 18. Early pregnancies and childbirth are the leading causes of death of adolescent girls in these countries.

Early forced marriage

Early forced marriage (also known as child marriage) happens when marriage is imposed on a child under the age of eighteen, often a girl made to marry a much older man. It is a form of sexual violence because the girls involved are unable to give or withhold their consent. Their first sexual encounters are therefore often forced on them. There is also a strong link with other types of abuse and domestic violence.

Every year at least 12 million girls – twenty-eight girls every minute – are married before they reach eighteen. They are then usually expected to have children as soon as possible, but pregnancy at a young age has a high risk of health complications. You are also likely to be pressured to drop out of school, limiting your education and your ability to escape poverty. Early forced marriage robs you of your right to make decisions about your own life.

In Yemen, 9% of girls are married before the age of fifteen. Many are taken out of school before they reach puberty. Yemen is the poorest country in the Middle East and the war (see Protection from armed violence, page 105) has driven people deeper into poverty and desperation. Early forced marriage is seen as a way of reducing household costs.

Maria lives in Burkina Faso. She was thirteen years old when her father forced her to marry a seventy-year-old man who already had five wives. Her father threatened to kill her if she resisted. Maria hadn't even had the chance to finish her first year of primary school or have a normal childhood. Three days after the wedding, she ran away, walking for more than three days to reach a centre for survivors of early forced marriage.

Boys are also affected, though in smaller numbers. Globally, one in thirty boys are married under the age of eighteen, compared with one in five girls. They too are forced to take on adult responsibilities. Marriage may bring early fatherhood and great pressure to provide for the household. It places barriers on getting a good education and career.

Child sex trafficking

Child trafficking happens in many forms (see Protection from harm, page 88), including for sexual exploitation and forced marriage. It is a global criminal enterprise that makes huge profits for traffickers and results in some of the most severe human rights abuses of children. It is a form of modern slavery and happens in all countries of the world, though the most common forms of trafficking vary in different places. In the Philippines an estimated 60,000 to 100,000 children a year are forced into sex work, many in tourist areas, after being promised service jobs such as being domestic helpers or entertainers.

Most of the time, children and young people are trafficked by someone they already know, like a friend, family member or romantic partner. Depending on your gender, you may be subject to different types of trafficking. Girls are more likely to be trafficked for early forced marriage and sexual exploitation, boys for forced labour. Many transgender/non-binary victims are trafficked for sexual exploitation. Sex trafficking in particular delivers enormous annual profits for the traffickers, while the victims earn nothing.

The use of online platforms to live-stream the sexual abuse of children is widespread, as paedophiles pay local traffickers and even families to abuse children. Extreme poverty and lack of education are often driving forces.

If you have been subjected to sexual exploitation, see Steps to take if you are being physically or sexually abused, page 178. Your rights have been abused by others and it is not your fault.

> Technology is increasingly being used in the fight against trafficking. Tech Against Trafficking is a coalition of technology companies collaborating with global experts. WeProtect is a global alliance led by the UK government and supported by a large number of countries, technology companies and **civil society** organisations, with the goal to end child sexual exploitation online. Other similar international platforms include the INTERPOL Specialists Group on Crimes Against Children and the Virtual Global Taskforce to Combat Child Online Exploitation.

Sexual and reproductive rights

Many abuses happen due to ignorance of rights, gender inequality and poverty. The situation is made far worse by lack of comprehensive sexuality education. You are at a much higher risk of female genital mutilation (cutting), early forced marriage and underage pregnancy if you are poor and if you don't have access to education. Social taboos against discussing sex and healthy relationships, together with a failure to provide sexual and reproductive health information, make you more vulnerable. So does the lack of protection given when you are using online platforms.

Comprehensive sexuality education (CSE) is described by the United Nations Educational, Scientific and Cultural Organisation (UNESCO) as 'an age-appropriate, culturally relevant approach to teaching about sex and relationships by providing scientifically accurate, realistic, non-judgemental information'. It has been found to boost young people's decision-making skills and to contribute to 'the prevention of unintended pregnancy, violence and abuse, and gender-based violence'.

Control over your sexual and reproductive choices often ends up in the hands of family members or religious groups. Governments and authorities have a duty to uphold equality, but some reinforce harmful stereotypes on the grounds of culture, tradition or religion. Many restrict education about sexual and reproductive rights and may try to control your rights over your own body.

FIGHT FOR RIGHTS
TAKING ACTION

Nicole de la Cruz is a teenage member of the child labour rights and social justice organisation MANTHOC in Peru. She has lived in a poor area on the outskirts of the capital Lima almost all her life. In Peru it is taboo to talk about young people's sexuality, and in Nicole's area many teenagers become pregnant and have had to drop out of school because of stigma.

In 2016, when Nicole was fourteen, she joined an education project on sexual and reproductive rights run by MANTHOC and Amnesty. It gave her training in educating other young people about their rights and the tools to promote comprehensive sex education at school.

The project meets with opposition from many in Peru's conservative society. But Nicole says:

> It's very important to teach young people to protect themselves and their bodies. I don't want to live in a society of submissive, battered, murdered women. I don't understand why there are people who don't want us to live in a society of respect, dignity and solidarity. I want us to be taught to respect all people from a young age, to implement comprehensive sex education and not to violate our rights.'

TAKING ACTION

FGM is illegal in Kenya, but a quarter of women and girls have undergone it. In 2017, five Kenyan teenage girls developed a ground-breaking app called 'iCut', which allows girls who are facing imminent FGM to alert the authorities by clicking a distress button on their mobile phone. The girls – Macrine Akinyi Onyango, Stacy Dina Adhiambo, Cynthia Awuor Otieno, Purity Christine Achieng and Ivy Akinyi, mentored by Dorcas Owinoh – named themselves 'The Restorers'.

Their app overcame some of the stigma about FGM and also provided resources to help girls who have undergone the process.

PROTECTION FROM ARMED VIOLENCE

Your right to life, survival and development means you have the right to be protected from armed conflict. You have the right to be supported if you've been hurt or badly treated. If you're underage, you should not be asked to fight or take part in hostilities.

From Articles 6, 37, 38, 39 and OP 1

WHAT DOES IT MEAN?

This upholds the General Principle to life, survival and development. The Convention says that children should be protected in situations of armed conflict. You should never be made to fight. If you are a child soldier, you have the right to special help to recover from trauma.

WHAT'S THE REALITY?

Throughout human history, children have been seriously affected by war. Armed conflicts are still rife around the world. Causes are complex, but nearly always include poverty and inequality.

Every government has the right and responsibility to manage their country's security and ensure public safety, in accordance with the rule of law. To do this well, it is legitimate for their armed and security forces to use a range of weapons. But those who buy and sell the weapons should guarantee they are transferred and stored safely, and that they don't end up in the wrong hands. Governments must ensure that arms in private ownership do not enter illicit circuits.

Armed conflicts everywhere are sustained by the international arms trade. Since 2014 there has been an international Arms Trade Treaty (ATT), which says that weapons should not be supplied in situations where they pose grave risks to human rights. Even so, the arms trade is often dangerously unregulated. The lack of regulation allows illegal or irresponsible trade to flourish, such as supplying arms that flout ATT and UN rules.

Every minute, war and armed conflict forces twenty people to leave their homes. Children are wounded, killed and orphaned. Schools and hospitals are targeted in bombing raids. Many children are recruited to fight. Rape, forced marriage and kidnap are used as standard tactics in many countries.

> By 2020, the war in Yemen had caused the deaths of around 100,000 people, including tens of thousands of children, from violence, hunger and disease. The coalition led by Saudi Arabia and the United Arab Emirates (UAE) has carried out many bombing raids and other attacks. It is said to be the greatest humanitarian disaster of the 21st century so far, and it is fuelled by the arms trade. Deaths of Yemeni people have been caused by bombs made in the US, UK and other countries and sold to the Saudi Arabia and UAE coalition.

Child soldiers

Child soldiers are young people under eighteen, who fight in armed conflicts. Some 300,000 children are thought to be fighting in conflicts around the world at any one time, and hundreds of thousands more are part of armed forces who could be sent into conflict. Most child soldiers are between the ages of fifteen and eighteen, but recruitment often starts around the age of ten, and the use of even younger child soldiers has been recorded.

Children become soldiers for many different reasons. Sometimes you are forcibly recruited – you might be taken out of your school or away from your community. You may join voluntarily, because you see the army as a safe place. Or you might join to receive food, clothing and shelter. If your family and friends are involved in the conflict, or have been killed, fighting might seem your only choice. But fighting has a major impact on children and young people. You can be wounded or permanently disabled, physically and psychologically. Witnessing and taking part in violence can also be very traumatic. Child soldiers usually need a lot of counselling and support after the conflict ends, but this is seldom available.

> In north-east Nigeria, conflict between the armed group Boko Haram and the Nigerian military began around May 2013. Both sides committed violence against children. Boko Haram repeatedly attacked schools and abducted large numbers of children as soldiers or 'wives', among other atrocities. The Nigerian military then committed further crimes against children who escaped Boko Haram. They imprisoned them unlawfully in inhumane conditions, beat them and allowed adult inmates to sexually abuse them. For those who returned home there was little or no support to help them recover or go to school.

Gun violence

Gun violence is violence committed with the use of firearms, such as pistols, shotguns, assault rifles or machine guns. It doesn't refer to warfare. Governments that fail to tackle and stop gun violence and gun deaths are not protecting child rights.

Even when a country is not at war, if the authorities permit easy access to guns, it can have a destructive impact on your life. This is especially the case if you live in a poor community. In the United States, the Second Amendment to the US Constitution of 1791 gives citizens the right to keep and bear arms. The combination of easy access to firearms and loose regulations lead to more than 39,000 people being killed with guns annually. Each year over 1,400 American children die through gun violence and an average of 5,790 children are given emergency treatment for gun-related injuries. Most of the child victims are from Black and minority communities. Unintentional shooting deaths and child suicides could be prevented through the implementation of Child Access Prevention laws that require guns to be stored safely and securely. However, 23 out of 50 US states have failed to enact any such laws.

In urban communities all over the world, gun violence by young people is linked to fear, a perceived need for protection that's not provided by the state, the distrust of police due to long-standing discrimination, and the desire for peer respect and approval. If you are made vulnerable by poverty and inequality, you may be easy prey for criminal gangs.

Globally, more than 500 people die every day from gun violence, including gangs and organised crime.

- There were 1.4 million deaths worldwide from gun violence between 2012 and 2016.

- In the United States, more than 25,000 children, including babies and toddlers, were killed by gun violence between 1999 and 2016.

FIGHT FOR RIGHTS
TAKING ACTION

Although I love Chicago, it's hard to live an everyday life here because we are "surviving". Joining BRAVE was one of the best decisions ever for me. It empowers me to change my community and potentially the city or the country, and it has brought out another side of me that others don't know about.'

Janaiya Alfred, aged 16

The city of Chicago in the United States has high rates of gun violence. Children pay a high price. In the first half of 2020, there were 440 murders. Twenty-four children

under the age of ten were shot, of whom five died. The impact on families of victims is immeasurable. In 2008 a peace programme for young people aged six to twenty-four was formed through St Sabina's Catholic Church on the south side of Chicago. It is called BRAVE, which stands for *Bold Resistance Against Violence Everywhere!*. In 2009 it created BRAVE Youth Leaders, a violence prevention youth council that trains young people to be peacemakers with their peers and leaders. It also gives them the opportunity to create change using leadership, peer to peer support, public speaking and activism. This after-school programme enables teenagers to combat the realities of everyday gun violence and social injustices. BRAVE's young people attend and speak at rallies, marches and discussions in and beyond Chicago.

Dealing with gun violence is something you go through every day, so there's really nothing to do but normalise it. The fact that gun violence is normalised is sick, because nobody seems to care these days. They're just used to it. Gun violence is like a part of our lives now. It's the new norm. BRAVE helps me voice my opinion more on this and other issues that no one seems to touch – like sex trafficking, single parent homes, abusive homes, depression and so on. It allows me to speak freely about how I feel – there are no wrong answers and it is a safe place to address any issues you may have. BRAVE gives you that solid foundation that you can depend on to back you up or have your back.'

Gabriel Kizer, aged 15

TAKING ACTION

Muhammad Najem was 15 years old in 2017 when he began to document the armed conflict in Syria. His father had been killed in an air strike on the mosque where he was praying. Muhammad witnessed extreme violence and suffering during the Syrian regime's siege of his village in Eastern Ghouta. He became determined to tell the world what was happening. Speaking in English to a Western audience, he used

social media to conduct interviews and document the day-to-day reality of life and death in a war zone. Whenever the bombing stopped, he and his older brother hurried to the rooftop and used a ten metre wi-fi pole with a USB stick to upload the footage. Soon Muhammad and his family were forced to flee. Eventually they were given asylum in Turkey, where he continues to report on ongoing war crimes and human rights abuses in his home country through contacts still in Syria.

TAKING ACTION

Ishmael Beah was born in 1980 in Sierra Leone, in West Africa, a country rich in natural minerals including diamonds. A civil war that lasted twelve years began in 1991, when rebels tried to overthrow the government. The country became unrecognisable through violence.

Both sides forcibly recruited child soldiers as cheap labour, killing the children if they didn't comply. They forced many to take part in murdering their own families and destroying their communities, so that no one would come looking for them and they wouldn't be able to return. It was a form of indoctrination. It also meant that child soldiers were no longer seen as children but feared as violent extremists.

When Ishmael was twelve, his family was killed and he fled from rebel soldiers. His world became one of fear; his long-term plans shrank to minute by minute survival. By the time he was thirteen, he had been picked up by the government army. It became his new family. Under its manipulative and coercive tactics, including the use of drugs, he found himself capable of committing terrible acts.

When he was fifteen he was rescued and taken to a UNICEF rehabilitation centre for child soldiers in Freetown, the capital. When he was sixteen, the civil war hit Freetown. He fled as a refugee to Guinea and eventually to the United States, where an American family adopted him. Since then he has used his voice to help change the course for thousands of children still trapped in wars.

In 2007 he became UNICEF's first Advocate for Children Affected by War. In 2008, he co-founded the Network of Young People Affected by War (NYPAW).

TAKING ACTION

Nigerian girl Oluwatomisin Jasmin Ogunnubi was twelve years old in 2015 when she developed a location tracking app to help lost children and young people find their way home. It was an innovative technological solution to the daily risks of violence 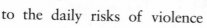 faced by young people and came at a time of nationwide insurgencies and reported cases of brutality by security forces. Records show that more than 30,000 children in Nigeria were separated from their parents or lost due to the Boko Haram armed conflict. In a country where emergency response is very limited, the My Locator app was designed to alert family members and emergency service units to the location of a lost young person, through a discreet press of a button on a mobile device.

Tomisin says:

'I wish I had realised earlier how much power we truly have in demanding and enforcing our rights. In my part of the world, people are quick to deem themselves helpless or simply "accept their fate" when their human rights are violated, especially by people in authority who propel the lies that nothing can be done about it. It is a lie we have allowed ourselves to be brainwashed with for a long time. I understand now that my rights are non-negotiable, and nobody should be given the luxury of denying them, regardless of their status. I also realise the power that we have in solidarity; speaking up for others and educating those who may be ignorant of their rights. I seek to empower others to know and stand up for their rights and to be the ally that every young girl needs in her corner. I stand in solidarity with every child all over the world.'

CRIMINAL JUSTICE AND LIBERTY

You have the right to be treated with dignity and worth. You cannot be punished in a cruel or harmful way. You are entitled to a fair hearing, with access to legal aid, and judges must consider your age and needs. You can only be deprived of your liberty as a measure of last resort and for the shortest appropriate time. You cannot be sentenced to death or life imprisonment without possibility of release for offences committed when you were under eighteen. You have the right to support to help you recover.

From Articles 37, 39 and 40

WHAT DOES IT MEAN?

This protects you and your childhood in two distinct ways, which often merge. It explicitly upholds the four General Principles (see page 25).

Article 40 looks at children in conflict with rules or the law. It says that you should not be judged as an adult, and you should be guaranteed a fair trial. If you have committed a crime, the focus should be on recovery, rehabilitation and reintegration into society, not punishment or retribution. Corporal (physical) punishment should not be used against children.

Governments should seek to prevent child crime by investing in areas where people live in great poverty. The Convention acknowledges that many crimes committed by children are the result of deep systemic issues that create or worsen poverty or psychological problems, and that you should not be treated as a criminal for running away, truancy or for living on the streets. Governments should also take measures to prevent discrimination against former child offenders, such as providing appropriate support and help to reintegrate in society.

It also says that children should not be deprived of liberty. Your right to life, survival and development (one of the General Principles) is integral. If your liberty is taken away from you, there is a serious impact on your development that also hampers your ability to reintegrate into society. Because of this, Article 37 says that **deprivation of liberty**, including arrest, detention and imprisonment, should be used only as an exceptional measure of last resort and for the shortest appropriate period of time. You must also not be put in a prison with adult offenders.

WHAT'S THE REALITY?

The reality is very different. Many governments violate Articles 37 and 40. Young people are often criminalised for minor offences, such as truancy, disobedience and underage drinking. Some countries, including Iran and South Sudan, treat children like adults if they are in conflict with the law, even handing out sentences of death, life imprisonment and corporal punishment. As of 2020, there were approximately 2,500 Americans serving life sentences without parole in the United States, for offences committed as a child.

There is a slow growth in the move against corporal punishment, where campaigners seek to give children the same protections as adults against smacking and other assault. By the end of 2020, 61 countries had completely banned it in all settings, including at home and school, while 28 others had made a commitment to reform their laws.

Sometimes countries wait for children to become adults before passing sentence, even though they were under eighteen at the time of the offence, and so should not be punished as adults. This is prohibited by international law, as is holding children in detention with adults, unless it is in the best interests of the child.

Being sent to prison is nearly always unnecessary and harmful to children. It is linked to anxiety, depression, suicidal thoughts and **post-traumatic stress**, which can be detrimental to your ability to think and reason.

It's estimated that over 7 million children around the world are deprived of their liberty each year. This means that they are held in some form of detention, imprisonment or custody, and that they cannot leave of their own free will. Of these, about 5.4 million are held in institutions (not criminal justice settings), including unregistered institutions, such as some 'orphanages' where many children are not actually orphans, and are at risk due to the lack of safeguards in place. Many children (at least 410,000) are held in prisons and pre-trial detention facilities, where violence is widespread. About a million more are held in other criminal justice settings, including police custody. The vast majority (94%) of children detained in the criminal justice context are boys. Children from racial or ethnic minorities, with disabilities, or living in poverty are more likely to be held in prisons and institutions.

At least 330,000 children are held in immigration detention in 80 countries every year, simply for being migrants or refugees. Many are forcibly separated from parents or families. This treatment makes you especially vulnerable to abuse and neglect. It is a complete violation of the Convention. In many cases it amounts to what is called 'cruel, inhuman or degrading' treatment of children.

In 2018, young people around the world sent thousands of solidarity messages to migrant children who had been unlawfully caged and separated from their families on the US/Mexico border. Most of the children had been fleeing persecution and violence in Central America, where their governments had not protected them. The solidarity messages helped to raise public awareness as well as letting the children know they were not forgotten. 'Freedom will come to you. Don't give up. We will be beside you whatever happens,' said a message written by a teenage girl in southern Thailand. A Venezuelan child drew a picture of a dog in a cage, with the message 'We are not animals.'

The Committee on the Rights of the Child encourages states to increase the minimum age of criminal responsibility to fourteen. You are not legally an adult until you reach the age of majority (eighteen in most countries), so you should not be judged as an adult. Your evolving capacities mean you are better able to understand cause and consequence of actions as you become more mature. But some countries criminalise children as young as six, whose 'offending' behaviour may be entirely normal for their developmental stage.

> As of October 2017, Madagascar held 785 children in prisons. Most of them were aged between fifteen and seventeen, but some were younger. In one prison Amnesty International visited, none of the children had ever met with a lawyer. The youngest was twelve years old, one of three boys held for theft of a chicken. He had already spent a month behind bars.

Regardless of a country's minimum age of responsibility, it is essential that anyone under eighteen is tried in accordance with child justice principles.

Examples of different ages of criminal responsibility:

- Australia – 10
- Brazil – 18
- Democratic Republic of Congo – no minimum
- Denmark – 15
- England and Wales – 10
- India – 7 (or 12 for a child who does not have sufficient understanding)
- Iran – 9 for girls, 15 for boys
- Nigeria – no minimum
- Peru – 18
- Saudi Arabia – 7
- South Africa – 10
- Thailand – 7
- US – varies from 6 to 10 across the states

FIGHT FOR RIGHTS
TAKING ACTION

Magai Matiop Ngong was fifteen years old when he was sentenced to death in South Sudan in 2017. He had taken his father's gun and fired it at the ground to scare away his cousin, who was trying to stop him fighting with another boy in his neighbourhood. But the bullet ricocheted and hit his cousin, who later died in hospital.

Magai did not have a lawyer to represent him during his trial. His death sentence was illegal by both international and South Sudanese law.

Amnesty helped to campaign for Magai. More than 765,000 people, including many children, sent protest messages to the South Sudanese president and solidarity messages to Magai himself. He was able to share his cards with others in his prison. In 2020 his death sentence was overturned but his cousin's family appealed the decision which means that his case will have to go back to court and the death sentence may be renewed.

Magai has gone through a huge transformation in prison and now refers to himself as 'Amnesty's ambassador'. People's solidarity helped save his life, but the impact goes much further. Magai is determined to dedicate his life to saving others through human rights work.

TAKING ACTION

In Belarus, thousands of children and young people are wrongly imprisoned for minor, non-violent drug offences. They serve long sentences in inhumane conditions.

In 2018, seventeen-year-old Vladislav Sharkovsky graduated from the school of the Olympic Reserve, where he had trained in Taekwondo. Both his parents lost their jobs so he started looking for work to help out. After a long search he was offered a job as a courier for an anonymous online company. He was repeatedly told that he was delivering legal smoking mixtures.

Two weeks later, he was arrested for 'illicit drug trafficking as part of an organised group'. He spent a night in a police station without his parents or a lawyer. He was beaten, pressured to write a statement and forced to give up his phone password. He was sentenced to ten years in prison for a minor, non-violent drug offence (later reduced to nine). No one else was prosecuted. Investigators didn't even try to find out the identity of the owner of the online company.

Vladislav's health deteriorated in prison but he wasn't allowed the medical care he needed. When Amnesty sent out an urgent appeal on his behalf in September 2019, many people around the world wrote letters of protest to the Belarusian authorities. He then received medical treatment. A second appeal resulted in more letters and his prison term was reduced by a year. The international solidarity has also helped his mental health:

> Global solidarity has meant the world to me. Knowing that you are not forgotten, and that other people stand up for your rights makes a big difference in prison.'

PRIVACY

You have the right to privacy and to be protected from bullying, harassment, threats and attacks on your reputation.

From Article 16

WHAT DOES IT MEAN?

This right protects your personal freedom and dignity and applies to all aspects of your life, including online. It says you should be able to live your life and interact with others as you want, without anyone (including the government) unfairly interfering or monitoring you. It lets you create safe boundaries and protects you from the abuse of individuals, governments, other state bodies and companies. It includes your right to stay secure online without being unjustly monitored or having your data collected, analysed or profiled.

WHAT'S THE REALITY?

Globally, in 2020 roughly 24 billion devices were connected with each other via the Internet. This makes you potentially vulnerable to abuse from an enormous range of actors – including governments, illegal networks, businesses and individuals.

Surveillance

Government **surveillance** is a targeted form of monitoring, usually without your knowledge or agreement. It is not only about gaining access to your information. It is also about control and intimidation, always forming part of a wider story of repression and human rights abuses. Governments are increasingly turning to surveillance techniques that violate the right to privacy. Russia has installed facial recognition systems to gather data about people who participate in public gatherings, including peaceful protests. China has advanced surveillance systems, even used to monitor children's facial expressions and attention levels in class. (If you are undertaking any activism, you need to keep yourself safe from surveillance. See Understand digital security, page 230.)

Illegal networks also use secret surveillance techniques. They can gain access to you through your devices, often wanting to exploit you for pornography and violence. Extremist groups gather information from social media platforms and try to radicalise vulnerable young people.

The United Kingdom's Metropolitan Police Service's gang-mapping database, known as the Gangs Matrix, was launched in 2012. It was part of a highly-politicised response to the 2011 London riots. The police's Gangs Unit monitored young people's behaviour online in order to gather data and determine possible gang affiliation. However, this was based on discriminatory views of young people. For example, sharing or liking grime music videos featuring gang names or signs was considered a possible indicator of likely gang affiliation. More than three-quarters (78%) of people on the Matrix were Black, a disproportionate number given that only 27% of those responsible for serious youth violence are Black. 80% were aged twelve to twenty-four.

Online abuse

Child abusers pretend to be your friends. They groom you, building what seems to be a genuine relationship, until you trust them. In reality, their purpose is to manipulate, exploit and abuse you, in person and often online. Abusers share your photos without your consent, sometimes through child abuse networks. This can seriously damage your mental and physical health, your reputation, and your relationships with friends and family. '**Trauma bonding**' refers to a very common ongoing emotional attachment between a victim and the person who has abused them. Remember, if this happens to you, you are not to blame, the abuse is not your fault, and the abuser has no rights over you. (See Steps to take if you are being physically or sexually abused, page 178.)

Cyberbullying happens when people bully and threaten you online. It's a form of casual cruelty that is often disguised as a joke, but recovery can be hard. It can be especially painful when others turn away and allow the bullying to happen. Victims can go on to struggle with eating disorders and mental and physical health issues, making it harder for them to concentrate in school or find jobs. Some bullies will target their victims by posing as a friend or boy/girlfriend. They extract intimate information or explicit photos from their victims, which they then share with the victim's wider social group. Sometimes they may circulate fake videos and photos that they have created themselves. The public humiliation can seriously damage young people's mental health. Recovery from such a betrayal of trust and abuse of privacy is hard.

There are also many positives to online activity and technology. You can petition for your cause, for example, and collect digital signatures and witness documentation. You can inform yourself by researching reliable sources of information. Telehealth is the delivery of healthcare from a distance via electronic communications and virtual technology. It helps the delivery of mental health support in times of war and health crises.

Corporate profiteering

Even apparently legitimate businesses can wield huge influence over your life without you knowing it. They use your personal devices to collect your private data, like your location, friendships, sexual orientation, political beliefs and health information, even your biometric data, such as fingerprints or voice recognition. With this, they can create a profile of you and aggressively market their goods to you. You may think you have free choice when you are shopping, but do you really? There is a long-term risk too. All this data, plus anything published by or about you online, is a permanent threat to your privacy and could be used against you in the future. Technology companies have the capacity to provide safe devices and platforms that protect children from harm, but it will likely take mass public pressure – including from young people – for them to deliver this.

FIGHT FOR RIGHTS
TAKING ACTION

Alex* is a student activist in Hong Kong, who was arrested in July 2020 under Hong Kong's new national security law. Alex had expressed their political opinion online, which was forbidden under the new law. They face possible life imprisonment because of some social media posts.

Alex began their activism in their early teens when they joined a school student organisation. Young people carried out protests and rallies, as well as designing and distributing activism posters and online infographics.

'We started to speak out publicly as a student group in the hope of getting more people, especially the young generation, to care about what was happening in society. Students should take responsibility for the future, as the future is ours . . . High school students in general know little about the society that we are living in, here in Hong Kong.

'When the law was passed, I became extremely cautious about what I posted online and I self-censored to avoid prosecution by the authorities, refraining from expressing something that could be deemed "unlawful". I removed pictures of my friends on Facebook and Instagram as I worried our connection would bring negative consequences to them. But I was arrested anyway, because of content posted on the student group's Facebook page. When I was released on bail, I stayed away from home for a few days, as I did not want my family to be filmed and interviewed. I was not prepared to face life imprisonment. I never imagined exercising my rights would cost me so much.

'My advice to young readers of this book is that it's crucial to be vigilant in protecting your digital identity. Make sure you do all necessary risk assessments before you take action. Also, study hard to become a person of influence in school or society in order to change the status quo. Nevertheless, someone has to make sacrifices for change to happen. It will take just one of us to stand up and act. Then, the rest of us will too. The Hong Kong movement has given me solidarity and hope. I know I am not alone in this.'

*Alex is not their real name but a pseudonym, to protect the activist's identity for fear of repercussions from the authorities.

MINORITY AND INDIGENOUS RIGHTS

You cannot be denied the right to enjoy
your own culture, practise your religion
and use your own languages if you belong
to a minority or Indigenous group.

From Article 30

WHAT DOES IT MEAN?

If you belong to a minority or Indigenous group, you
have the same rights as all other children. Article 30
places a duty on your government not to discriminate
against you and to stop organisations and authorities
such as schools from doing so. No one is allowed to
use hate speech against you.

You are Indigenous if your ancestors are the original
people of a place. You are likely to have unique
languages, knowledge systems and beliefs, with a
special relationship to your ancestral land.

You belong to a **minority group** if your ethnicity,
race, language or religion are different to those of the
dominant group in your country. The term 'minority
group' doesn't necessarily mean there are fewer of

you. It means you're part of a group that is subjected to oppression and discrimination by those in power. Even if there are fewer of you, it does not give the 'majority' the right to oppress you in any way. Groups who have been referred to as minorities include Black Americans, women, immigrants and Gypsy, Roma and Traveller people. Most Indigenous people are also in minority groups.

WHAT'S THE REALITY?

There are about 5,000 minority groups in the world, spread across nearly every country. Children from Indigenous and minority groups routinely face discrimination. They may have to repress their identity, their history is unlikely to be taught in schools, they may not be able to speak their own language freely or enjoy their culture's traditions. For centuries, minorities have been victims of scapegoating, persecution and even genocide.

If you belong to a minority group, your country's majority or ruling population is likely to see you as 'different'. As you grow up, you may often be excluded from your country's ways of doing things. For example, more than half of children excluded from school around the world are from minority or Indigenous groups. There are many possible consequences, such as being more likely to experience long-term poverty and your government paying less attention to your needs.

Since 2017, China has imposed a 'Strike Hard against Violent Terrorism Campaign', which actually targets minority groups for their faith, ethnicity and culture. It has involved the unlawful detention and imprisonment of about a million Uyghur and other Turkic Muslims, who are minority groups living mostly in Xinjiang province in north-western China. People are labelled 'extremist' if they refuse to watch state television, or have an 'abnormal' beard, wear a veil or headscarf, pray regularly, fast or avoid alcohol. Children have been forcibly separated from their parents and sent to state-run child welfare institutions and boarding schools. They are not allowed to contact their parents. Many of their other rights are also violated, including their right to speak their own language and know their cultural heritage. Numbers are not known, because of intense government control and surveillance, with severe punishments for anyone who speaks out.

About 400 minority languages have become extinct in the last century. Languages usually reach crisis point when they are displaced by another language that is used by a dominant group of people. Speaking the dominant language then becomes essential for you to access education, jobs and other opportunities. Sometimes parents decide not to teach children their heritage language in case it hinders them in life. The situation is made far worse by the persecution of people who speak minority languages.

This is important because language is intricately tied up with being human. Your language is deeply personal. It is often the only way to communicate traditions, songs, unique pieces of knowledge and experience that happen nowhere else in the world. When languages and cultures die, humankind suffers an irretrievable loss. There are now more than 570 languages listed as critically endangered, with thousands more categorised as endangered or threatened. The highest numbers are in the Americas.

Another challenge you may face if you belong to a minority or Indigenous group is accessing your right to education. This has been the case for a long time. In Wales from the 18th to early 20th centuries, if school children spoke their native Welsh language instead of English (the language of the dominant colonisers), they were routinely punished. A piece of wood inscribed with 'Welsh Not' was hung around their necks. Decades of protest eventually led to Welsh being made compulsory in all schools in Wales. Now, nearly a quarter of the population of Wales speaks Welsh.

In the Czech Republic children from the minority Roma community have long faced daily discrimination in school. They are often segregated in Roma-only separate classes and buildings or placed in separate schools. They may be labelled as having 'mild mental disabilities' simply because they belong to a minority group. Roma children in ethnically mixed schools often experience bullying and harassment.

In 1837 the British government imposed 'assimilation' on Indigenous people living in British colonies. The aim was to strip them of cultures and languages that were regarded as inferior. In Canada, Australia and New Zealand, residential schools were created. The United States, no longer a British colony, did likewise. The residential schools forcibly assimilated Indigenous children into Western culture.

Many children didn't see their families again for many years, if ever. Children were punished for speaking their native languages or observing any Indigenous traditions. They were physically and sexually assaulted on a routine basis. Some were subjected to medical experimentation and sterilisation. The forced removals continued for nearly 150 years. Not until 1978 were Indigenous American parents given the legal rights to refuse school placement for their children.

The lasting impact on Indigenous communities is immeasurable. Thousands of children died. If they survived, they lost their families, sacred traditions and their cultural identity. The Canadian government has officially called the residential school system a cultural genocide.

FIGHT FOR RIGHTS
TAKING ACTION

Indigenous and tribal people live on roughly 25% of land on Earth, in territories that are rich in biodiversity and home to 80% of plant and animal life. These areas are highly vulnerable to climate change and toxic waste. Protecting Indigenous lands is essential in the fight to save the planet as well as human and child rights.

Tokata (Future) Iron Eyes is a member of the Standing Rock Sioux tribe in the United States. When she was

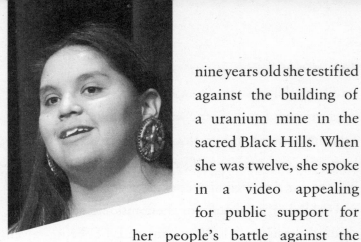

nine years old she testified against the building of a uranium mine in the sacred Black Hills. When she was twelve, she spoke in a video appealing for public support for her people's battle against the proposed route of the Dakota Access oil pipeline. 'Respect our water, respect our land and respect our people. Join us and sign our petition,' she said. The campaign helped draw thousands of national and international visitors to Standing Rock to fight the pipeline in a protest that lasted nearly a year. The pipeline was installed, but the tribe continues to fight.

In 2020, aged sixteen, Tokata Iron Eyes joined the board of a new sustainable energy group called Indigenised Energy. She continues to advocate for the planet and Indigenous rights.

> By living your truth and recognising the world's suffering, you are already a part of the change. Trust yourself – and be loud about it.'

TAKING ACTION

In Australia's schools, the teacher training and curriculum is filled with white settler language, history, literature, mathematics, science and culture. The lack of representation of Indigenous children makes it hard for Aboriginal and Torres Strait Islanders to feel valued or included. Some express their frustration through resistance. Often, instead of being given support, the children are subject to surveillance from police and child welfare systems.

Discrimination also happens outside school. Only 6% of Australia's ten to seventeen-year-olds are Indigenous, but they make up 54% of children in prison. They are twenty-five times more likely to be in prison than non-Indigenous children. They have also been subjected to abuse and torture such as isolation, restraint chairs, spit hoods, tear gas and invasive search procedures.

What I want is a normal life of just being me. And what I mean by me is: I want to be an Aborigine.'

Dujuan Hoosan is an Arrernte and Garrwa boy from Australia. He has a strong connection to his culture,

speaks three languages and is recognised as a healer, an important position in his community. But the skills and intelligence he has inherited from his people are not valued or included in the Australian schooling system. He has experienced serious discrimination, such as being excluded from school and threatened with prison. In the Northern Territory, where he lives, 100% of children in prison in 2020 were Indigenous.

Dujuan's life experiences were shown in a documentary film called *In My Blood It Runs*. In 2019, when he was twelve, Dujuan travelled to Geneva and became the youngest person ever to address the UN Human Rights Council and the UN Committee on the Rights of the Child. He called for Australia to raise the age of criminal responsibility from ten to fourteen, and spoke about his own experiences of nearly entering Australia's youth justice system. He also spoke about the need to rebuild education systems led by Aboriginal people.

> Adults never listen to kids – especially kids like me. But we have important things to say.'

Dujuan's story has been shared many thousands of times through his speech and screenings of the film. He has helped Australia refocus on Indigenous children and communities and to better understand that children have the right to participate in all decisions that affect them.

EDUCATION

You have the right to an education and schooling to help develop your personality, talents and abilities. You have the right to information and guidance. You have the right to know your rights.

From Articles 13, 17, 28, 29 and 42

WHAT DOES IT MEAN?

You should have an education. This is vital to your own personal development and can be key in escaping poverty. It is also part of creating a more inclusive, sustainable and progressive society. Primary education must be compulsory, free and equally accessible to all children. All governments should take measures to provide secondary and vocational education on a free basis. School discipline can only be administered in ways that respect your dignity. You can never be hit at school. Under the Convention, you should be educated in the spirit of peace, tolerance, equality and friendship amongst all peoples.

WHAT'S THE REALITY?

When the Convention was adopted in 1989, 120 million children were missing a primary education.

Great progress was made and by 2017 this number had fallen to less than 64 million. Yet in 2019 roughly one in five children and young people still didn't go to primary school, with girls more likely than boys never to enrol. The United Nations has set a goal of achieving universal primary education by 2030.

> The global Covid-19 pandemic stopped about a billion children and young people from attending school in 2020, with experts predicting that up to 10 million children might never return to school. But if you do not receive an education, you cannot become the nurses, doctors, scientists and health experts that the world will need to solve future epidemics.

Primary education should be free and compulsory for every child. But being able to go to school doesn't necessarily mean you receive a decent education. It is very hard to learn if your school has few trained teachers or resources, for example, or makeshift and overcrowded classes in run-down buildings and inadequate sanitation facilities. In sub-Saharan Africa, fewer than half of primary and lower secondary schools (for young people aged roughly twelve to fifteen) have access to drinking water, electricity, computers or the Internet. Given this, it's not surprising that about

617 million young people around the world don't reach minimum standards in literacy or maths.

It's also hard to learn if you are hungry, sick or tired from working outside school. It's even harder if you have to walk for hours just to get to school, maybe navigating minefields or people who want to harm you. You may be one of 27 million children who can't get to school because they are struggling to survive in a war zone.

There are many reasons why children are excluded from schools. If you have a disability or are from an ethnic minority, you'll tend to find it much harder to get an education. Gender discrimination means that in 44% of countries girls don't have equal access to primary education. If you're from a poor household, you are nearly five times more likely to be out of school than if you're from a wealthy family. According to a UNICEF report from 2016, in many countries, students growing up in the richest households had access to up to eighteen times more public educational resources, including textbooks and other materials, than students from the poorest households.

You also have the right to know your rights, which is why we've made this book. Yet some schools prioritise formal teaching, such as learning by rote, over critical thinking. One of the benefits of developing critical thinking and questioning skills is that it helps you find out the truth. In so doing, you are better equipped to know and claim your rights.

> Being excluded from books is another obstacle to learning and development. *Reflecting Realities* is an annual survey of children's books published in the UK. Between 2017 and 2019, 7% of children's books featured ethnic minority characters, set against a national school population where 33% of children were of ethnic minority origins. Yet stories are crucial to education and better life chances. They support freedom of thought and can help equality and justice to flourish. If children don't find themselves in a book, they can be discouraged from reading and find education harder as a result.

FIGHT FOR RIGHTS
TAKING ACTION

In 2002, in West Bengal, India, Babar Ali started teaching when he was nine years old. When he returned home from school each day he shared what he had learned with local children who couldn't go to school and had to work instead. His backyard became the school. There was no roof or seating area, so when it rained, classes had to be cancelled, but the children were not put off. What started as a game became very serious. Babar's parents supported the right to education, but the other parents were mistrustful – especially if their child was a girl.

Even so, by 2015, Babar's backyard school had grown so much it had to move. It was also recognised by the West Bengal School Education Department. It now has more staff, and by 2020 it had taught about 5,000 children (60% of them boys and 40% girls) from poor families without charge.

> I'd see girls and boys of my age coming home from work instead of coming home from school. I would make them sit in the backyard of our home and teach them. I was the headmaster. I did not give up. I fought tooth and nail and when I founded this school, parents were very sceptical about educating their children. They were not educated

themselves so they did not realise the value of education. We went door to door to send their kids to school. Now my students are starting in college. Some of them are now teaching at my school.'

TAKING ACTION

Since the 1990s parts of Pakistan and Afghanistan have experienced control by the Taliban, a hardline militant Islamic group. From 2007 to 2009, the Taliban targeted Swat Valley in the north of Pakistan – banning girls' education, bombing schools and preventing women from going outside their houses.

> If one girl can change the world, what can 130 million do?'

An 11-year-old girl from Swat Valley, Malala Yousafzai, began speaking out for girls' right to education. From writing an anonymous blog for the BBC to speaking to the local and international media about the urgency of action for peace and protection, Malala started her activism in a time of dire need and crisis in her area. She wanted to continue her education and help other girls do the same. Malala, along with her father Ziauddin Yousafzai, attracted international media attention and won awards for their activism.

In 2012, when she was fifteen, Malala was shot in the head by the Taliban for speaking out. She recovered due to the treatment she received in Pakistan and the UK. She continued her fight for girls and her call for education grew  into a worldwide movement. In Pakistan, over 2 million people signed a petition pressuring the government to introduce the Right to Education Act – making girls' education more widely accessible. The National Assembly also ratified Pakistan's first Right to Free and Compulsory Education Bill.

In 2013, Malala and Ziauddin co-founded Malala Fund, a nonprofit organisation working to ensure every girl can access twelve years of free, safe, quality education. The following year, in recognition for her work, Malala became the youngest person ever to be awarded the Nobel Peace Prize. She was seventeen. She has since graduated with a degree in Philosophy, Politics and Economics at Oxford University.

With more than 130 million girls out of school around the world, Malala continues to dedicate her life to fighting for a future where all girls can learn and lead.

TAKING ACTION

Heidy Quah was a sixteen-year-old school student in Petaling Jaya in Malaysia when she started volunteering at a refugee school. As she got to know the children there, she began to appreciate the  many challenges their families faced and how different her own life and expectations about education were, even though they were growing up in the same country. When she found out the school's funding was under threat, she had the idea to set up her own non-governmental organisation (NGO) to help refugees access basic education facilities.

Within eight years, Heidy had founded ten refugee schools across Malaysia and twenty-five schools across Myanmar, providing a schooling system with a strong emphasis on leadership development for over 2,000 children. Today, the scope of her work has expanded. She now also provides holistic support to vulnerable people in her community who are being exploited or having their rights violated. She makes sure they receive healthcare, safety and protection while she works with the authorities to seek justice.

I grew up thinking that privilege meant big fancy cars, or staying in a nice house, or going on luxurious holidays with my family. When I started working with the community, I learned that privilege simply meant having access to education, having a roof over my head, being able to walk out of the house and not worry about my safety and not needing to worry about when my next meal was. With that, I was determined to use whatever little resources I had, to ensure that the communities I served would get access to basic human rights. By the time I was eighteen, it was this understanding of my privilege that inspired me to set up Refuge For The Refugees.'

PLAY

You have the right to play, rest, choose your own friends, share ideas and enjoy cultural and artistic activities.

From Article 31

WHAT DOES IT MEAN?

At the heart of children's lives everywhere is the right to play, including games, sport and the creative arts, such as drama, dance, art, music and poetry. It supports your right to a voice and to agency and it is vital to your health and well-being.

The right to play helps your development in every way – physical, intellectual, social and emotional – and is a form of self-expression. It is a creative way to experience and explore the world around you and to develop skills for life. It gives you control of what you do and helps you learn to manage risk, stay safe and make decisions. It's unifying – possibly the best way to make friends and learn how to communicate and how to listen. Many games are rooted in cultural traditions, so can be part of shaping and understanding your identity. Play is fun, creative, spontaneous, flexible and non-productive. It challenges you but helps you unwind. It shouldn't need much (if any) equipment as there isn't a right to toys. Play helps your mind and imagination flourish, which is vital to constructing a better world. As you grow older, the ways in which you relax and interact with your friends may change, but they are just as important.

This right obliges governments to ensure that every child has the opportunity to play, rest, relax, and enjoy sports and cultural and artistic activities in a safe environment.

WHAT'S THE REALITY?

The right to play can be restricted by adults who see it as an unnecessary indulgence, inferior to other forms of education. In many countries, children report wanting more playtime.

Many children say that well-being and happiness centres on having good friends and plenty to do outdoors. But there are many barriers. On a basic level, these include risks such as playing near busy roads, pollution, bullying and discrimination. Some adults may not understand how important play is for your lifelong learning and development. Schools tend to focus on formal teaching rather than playtime and time outdoors. They often stop local children from using school playgrounds during out-of-school hours.

Most modern streets were not built with children in mind, so street conditions in many places are unwelcoming and dangerous. According to the World Health Organisation, in 2018 road crashes were the leading cause of death worldwide for young people between the ages of five and twenty-nine. Noisy and unsafe streets discourage play or independent activity. This in turn is bad for your physical and mental health as well as your cognitive function (your thinking ability). Much of this is preventable.

In 2020, the Global Designing Cities Initiative launched 'Designing Streets for Kids'. Its approach to designing urban streets puts people first, with a focus on the specific needs of babies, children and their caregivers. Countries taking on this approach include Albania. Its capital city Tirana adapted the main traffic-dominated Skanderbeg Square in close consultation with local children. The square transformed from a hostile, traffic-dominated environment to somewhere much friendlier, with car-free days to encourage walking and cycling.

If you are living in crisis and struggling to access your other rights – perhaps because of abuse, conflict or poverty – creative play becomes an even more important way to help you overcome stress and build resilience.

> Where authorities respect children's right to a voice, there are dramatic benefits for equal access to play. In Wales and Sweden, for example, children are consulted on the building of new playgrounds. Adapted swings have also been built to ensure children with disabilities get the same opportunities to play as everyone else.

FIGHT FOR RIGHTS
TAKING ACTION

On the outskirts of Paraguay's capital city Asunción is the district of Cateura. It is the largest and poorest slum area in Paraguay and is home to a giant rubbish dump. About 40,000 people live here, in extreme poverty. The water is polluted, sewage runs down the street and the river often floods. There is a constant sour smell and little wildlife. Rubbish is the main import and way of life. 40% of the children who live here never finish school because they are needed to work for their families. In 2006, thanks to the vision of a student of human ecology engineering who had musical training, combined with the support of community waste pickers, local children and young people began to learn to play music. Together, they took some of the rubbish, turned it into musical instruments, and formed the Paraguayan Recycling Youth Orchestra. The instruments were made from forks, X-rays, pipes, coins, wooden crates and more. The orchestra now plays music on international stages. Music and creative play have transformed these children's lives.

TAKING ACTION

' There was a bad image of Tripoli because of the war – only conflict and violence. Now we play football to learn about cooperation, helping each other and staying out of trouble.'

Said is a seventeen-year-old refugee in Lebanon. He lives in an informal settlement called Al Quobbeh, just outside the city of Tripoli, that is home to displaced Palestinian, Syrian and Lebanese families. Life here is tough and Said was bullied as a child, but when he was eleven he joined a sport for development programme run by the international organisation Right To Play, which brings children together through sport and teaches them to cooperate. It was transformative. The programme helped him deal with his trauma and to heal. Keen to help other children from poor and disadvantaged backgrounds, he became a football coach himself and used the techniques 'he learned from Right To Play.

At the beginning of 2019 just ten children showed up at his sessions. By 2020 numbers had grown to over thirty.

FREEDOM OF THOUGHT

You have the right to freedom of thought,
conscience and religion, so long as it doesn't
interfere with other people's rights and
the safety, security and health of society.
You can choose to follow any faith or none.
Your parents have the right to guide you.

From Article 14

WHAT DOES IT MEAN?

This is one of the Convention's participation rights,
closely linked to your right to freedom of expression.
It is a more limited right than adults have, because it
allows your parents to guide you as you grow so that
you are not harmed. But it still grants you the right
to freedom of thought, conscience and religion. It
says you shouldn't be discriminated against on the
basis of your religion, nor if you are a non-believer. It
provides you with intellectual and spiritual freedoms
so that your mind can grow and develop. It allows
you to refuse to participate in activities with which
you disagree, such as joining the armed forces, eating
meat or drinking alcohol. If you are a non-believer, it
is your right to refuse to take part in religious worship.

This right lays a foundation for you to imagine and shape a better world.

It also acknowledges the role played by the mosque, church, synagogue, temple or other religious and spiritual meeting places in your community. These can be important places for you to learn moral values and make friends. A religious community can help you become part of a collective identity. It can help you feel part of the world.

WHAT'S THE REALITY?

No one should suffer discrimination because of their faith or non-faith, yet religious minorities are some of the most vulnerable in society. In some cases, religion can quite literally be a matter of life or death. People of faith are persecuted all over the world, usually by those claiming to uphold other religions. Persecution is also inflicted on people who have converted from one faith to another or who are atheists. It is often driven by political motives, ambition, aggression or greed.

More than 80% of people live in countries where there are restrictions on what you can believe. If there is a connection, or intersection, between your religious and ethnic identity, it can make you more vulnerable, especially if you are not part of a country's dominant group. Many children face discrimination at school because of religion or belief. If low-level abuse of individuals – for wearing a headscarf or crucifix, for example – is left unchecked, it can quickly escalate. The Holocaust (see page 15) followed centuries of anti-Semitism, the term used to describe prejudice against and hatred of Jewish people. From 1933 on, the German Nazi party used propaganda, persecution, and legislation to deny human and civil rights to Jews across the entire continent of Europe. By 1945, they had murdered 6 million Jewish people, as well as others whose identities or religious beliefs conflicted with their ideology.

Genocide is the deliberate attempt to murder as many people as possible belonging to a national, ethnic, racial or religious group. **Crimes against humanity** includes crimes like murder, rape and persecution committed as part of a planned widespread and systematic attack against a civilian population.

Freedoms of belief, expression and peaceful assembly (the right to meet and express yourself with others) are closely linked, but there is often a tension between them and with other rights. Some religions repress homosexuality, for example. Many repress gender equality. The right to faith can be misused as a tool of oppression.

> In Pakistan, so-called blasphemy laws are often used to persecute religious minorities and others who are targeted with false accusations. Rimsha Masih, a Christian girl with a learning disability, was fourteen years old in 2012 when she was accused of blasphemy by a local cleric. He said she had burned pages of the Qur'an. Despite being a child with a disability, she was arrested by the police and charged. After a three-month ordeal in the glare of the media, the Islamabad High Court quashed the charge, saying that she had been falsely implicated without any evidence. Rimsha and her family fled to Canada, where they were given asylum because of the threats they faced.

FIGHT FOR RIGHTS
TAKING ACTION

In 1992, the eastern European republic of Bosnia declared independence from Yugoslavia. Bosnia's population at the time was ethnically mixed. The creation of an independent Bosnian nation with a Bosnian Muslim majority was bitterly opposed by Bosnian Serbs, who started a war to win territory and 'cleanse' Bosnia of its Muslim population. In order to gain political domination they were prepared to carry out war crimes and mass killings of ethnic groups in a process that became known as '**ethnic cleansing**'. The civil war lasted from 1992 to 1995 and led to the first genocide in Europe since the Holocaust. An estimated 100,000 people were killed, 80% of whom were Bosnian Muslims. Over 2 million men, women and children were displaced.

Zlata Filipović was a ten-year-old Bosnian child at the time. She wrote a diary about living through the war in her city of Sarajevo and described how her friends and family were suddenly labelled by their ethnicity or faith, of  which she had been unaware. Her diary was turned into a book and published in 36 languages around the world.

Zlata grew up to become a professional writer and film producer. She says of her childhood, 'One of the great tools that helped me during my time as a child growing up during the siege of Sarajevo was writing. Being able to put down my thoughts and feelings on a non-judgemental listening piece of blank paper; having to find verbs and nouns for the jumble in my head and in my heart – it really was a support through those difficult times (and beyond!).'

TAKING ACTION

Sixteen-year-old Rozia Bibi lives with her mother in Cox's Bazar in Bangladesh, the world's largest refugee settlement. Rozia is a Rohingya Muslim from Myanmar. Her father was murdered during an episode of Myanmar's violent 'ethnic cleansing' against the Rohingya, which began in 2017 and forced 700,000 people to flee across the border into Bangladesh. In majority-Buddhist Myanmar, the government has committed extreme and severe rights violations against the Rohingya Muslim people, who are from a minority group and represent the largest percentage of Muslims in Myanmar.

Over half of the Rohingya refugees in Cox's Bazar are women and girls. Extreme poverty forces many young girls into early (often violent) marriage and motherhood. Desperate to protect her daughter,

Rozia's mother Anwara Begum sold some jewellery and bought a sewing machine. Rozia and her mother now work as tailors in the camp, training other women and young girls so they are not forced to marry. Rozia advocates for the rights of all Rohingya children to have access to education, so they can obtain skills, independence and a brighter future.

VOICE AND PEACEFUL PROTEST

You have the right to freedom of expression, peaceful protest and peaceful assembly. You are entitled to seek out and find information.

From Articles 13 and 15

WHAT DOES IT MEAN?

This upholds the Convention's General Principle on your rights to be heard, to participate and to be listened to. Freedom of expression – including free speech – means you are entitled to seek, receive and share information and ideas of all kinds, by any means, including through the arts. You shouldn't be blocked or censored. You can use your voice in acts of solidarity with others as well as in peaceful protest.

'Peaceful assembly' means you have the right to gather together with friends and others for peaceful protest. You have this right on an equal basis with adults and are entitled to it without being discriminated against on the basis of your age or anything else.

Governments should implement special measures to protect you during a peaceful assembly, but not in a way that restricts your freedom of expression. You should be aware that in some situations they are permitted to restrict the right to freedom of expression. This is because they also have obligations to ban hate speech and incitement to violence, to protect people and uphold national security.

Your right to a voice, to express yourself, extends beyond speaking. It includes writing, creating art, making music, openly respecting others' rights, upholding equality, mobilising protest and much more. You can use your voice to resist oppression and spread knowledge and ideas. You can call for change, in small ways and big. You can use it for yourself and in solidarity with others.

Most of the true stories in this book are about young people who have used the right to a voice and peaceful protest and have acted in solidarity with others.

WHAT'S THE REALITY?

The right to a voice means you have the right to be listened to. But people can choose not to listen. And authorities tend to be afraid of the power of people's voices to articulate and achieve social change. They frequently clamp down on the right to freedom of expression and peaceful protest. Around the world, journalists, artists and writers are often censored – or silenced – through means that include imprisonment and murder. It's usually because of their skill in expressing ideas and stirring emotions. **Censorship** arises out of a fear of change and the potential loss of power.

You are likely to face various constraints to your enjoyment of the right to peaceful assembly. Your parents may not give consent, or there may be restrictive school rules and local laws. Nonetheless, your right to peaceful assembly is protected in international law and in some national bills of rights, so governments should remove obstacles that stop you enjoying this right, such as laws that set a minimum age for organising or participating in peaceful assemblies, laws requiring parental consent to join associations and laws that allow the police to remove children who assemble peacefully in groups. The police's role and responsibility is not to clamp down on your rights, but to uphold them and protect you.

FIGHT FOR RIGHTS
TAKING ACTION

' I started journalism at the age of seven because I wanted the whole world to know what is happening here and how we live in fear and uncertainty. I faced a lot of situations, like seeing my relatives killed in front of me, my mother being injured, my friends getting arrested. I want a normal life, a normal childhood.'

Janna Jihad grew up in the small Palestinian village of Nabi Salih. It is located north of Ramallah city on the West Bank, part of the Palestinian territory that has been under Israel's military occupation since 1967. Palestinian children and their communities are denied their rights and face discrimination on a daily basis. The Israeli army arrests children from Janna's village regularly, often when raiding their homes in the middle of the night while families are asleep. The children struggle

169

to access their rights to education and freedom of movement. Barriers and checkpoints force delays on any journey, so it can take hours to get to school instead of a few minutes. People find it hard to travel to work and earn a living to support their families. For anyone who is sick, it can be nearly impossible to get to hospital.

In 2009, when Janna was three, her community used their right to peaceful protest and began weekly demonstrations. They were met with violence. When she was seven, Janna's uncle and her friend were killed by the Israeli military. She used her mother's phone to record what was happening and reveal the truth. In essence, she became a human rights reporter. By the time she was a teenager, her live videos were watched by hundreds of thousands of people around the world. She faced many threats for her work.

In 2019 Janna became the youngest press card-carrying journalist in the world at the age of thirteen.

TAKING ACTION

Annie Alfred is like any other child in Malawi, except that she was born with albinism, an inherited condition that stops her body from making enough colour,

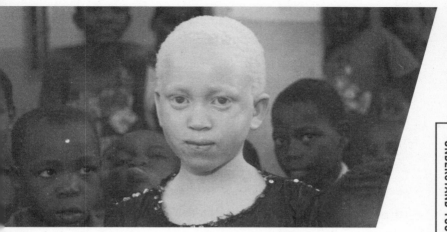

or melanin, to protect her skin from the sun. She is put at great risk by people who believe her body has magic powers. These people think she's not human. They want to steal her hair or bones and sell them for money. About 7,000 to 10,000 people in Malawi have albinism. They are all at risk of being killed by people who think their body parts will make them rich.

People call me Ghost. Because I have albinism. But I am just like anyone else. Just with white skin and white hair. But some people think that my bones and hair have magic powers that give them money and power. And they will do anything to get them.'

Annie lived in extreme poverty with her grandmother, in an area with many criminal gangs. They couldn't afford for her to go to school. In 2016, when she was eight, she agreed to be part of Amnesty's annual Write for Rights campaign.

Many thousands of young people around the world sent solidarity and protest cards. Malawi's president received 10,000 messages telling him to take action to end the attacks. The solidarity actions achieved a swift result. Within a few months, Malawian authorities changed the law. Now anyone caught with the bones or body parts of a person with albinism faces life in jail. As for Annie, she was supported to go to a safe and protected boarding school for young people with albinism.

TAKING ACTION

In September 2020, a group of four children and two young adults from Portugal filed a climate change case with the European Court of Human Rights in Strasbourg. They accused governments of endangering their futures by failing to reduce emissions. They brought the case against thirty-three countries with the support of the Global Legal Action Network. They succeeded in getting crowd-funding to pay for the legal action, which centred on the threat that climate change poses to their lives and to their physical and mental well-being. They hope to tackle the international responsibility for climate change and to force countries to reduce emissions quickly.

Sofia Oliveira, aged fifteen, said:

> We have seen unbearable heatwaves that cause water shortages and damage food production, and violent wildfires that give us anxiety and make us afraid to travel through our country's forests . . .
> If we already see these extremes in 2020, what will the future be like?'

PART THREE

CLAIM YOUR YOUR RIGHTS

'Get up, stand up, stand up for your rights. Get up, stand up, don't give up the fight.'

From 'Get Up, Stand Up' by Bob Marley, Jamaican singer and songwriter, 1973

FIRST STEPS

As you can see, having rights doesn't mean all children and young people can access them. Knowledge is the starting point. You are entitled to claim your rights, but for some of you it will be dangerous, depending on your personal circumstances and where you live. You should be very careful. People have been harmed and have died claiming their basic rights.

Claiming child rights is likely to mean challenging national laws or local rules that are preventing you from enjoying them. It may require you to raise awareness and to seek changes in political and public systems. For some of you, the abuse may be close to home and dangerous to confront.

This part includes information about approaches to claiming rights that have worked for others. You may want to adapt some of them and make them your own, or you might want to act in solidarity with others. None of this is easy. The most important thing is to keep yourself safe, both physically and mentally.

CHECK YOUR PHYSICAL SECURITY

If you are claiming your rights, you are facing risks. You must be careful not to endanger yourself or others. You need to think carefully about not just your physical safety, but also digital security (page 230) and mental health (page 244). This is crucial.

- Will claiming your rights put you or anyone else at risk?

- What are the potential risks and dangers? Think through them all.

- Could your actions jeopardise your relationship with your family?

- Could you face repercussions in school, in the community or in your workplace (if you have one)?

- Is there anyone who would try and hurt you?

If the answer to any of these is *yes*, you need to consider your course of action very carefully. Do you have someone you trust whom you could talk to? Think through all the possible scenarios and try to work out if different actions would help to avoid some risks. It's really important to do thorough planning in advance of taking action and not to do anything that might threaten your physical safety.

STEPS TO TAKE IF YOU ARE BEING PHYSICALLY OR SEXUALLY ABUSED

It is vital to speak out if you – or someone you know – is being physically or sexually abused. Sexual abuse is traumatic, especially if the abuser is someone you look up to or care about. You may not want to make them angry or get them into trouble. But abusers are manipulative: they will try to make you feel special, fearful or complicit. They rely on trauma bonding (which keeps you emotionally attached to an abuser) to sustain their influence over you, sometimes for many years. If more than one person is involved or the abuse has been going on for a long time, you may have been made to feel like it's normal.

Here are some steps you can take.

- It may feel like it is your fault, but it really isn't. The crime has been committed by someone else. Their abuse goes way beyond the physical to the psychological and emotional and they deliberately try to make you feel responsible. Forgive yourself, in your head and your heart.

- Don't keep the abuse or the abuser secret. Find someone you trust to talk to. This might be a family member, a friend, a teacher, a nurse or doctor, someone in your community. Many countries have a free dedicated childline you can call confidentially.

- This can be hard, especially if you feel ashamed or the abuser threatens you. Remember, you have nothing to be ashamed of because it is not your fault. The abuser's threats need to be dealt with. Talking about it will help you practically and emotionally. You should also seek support for any feelings of self-blame.

- If the person you trust doesn't listen, lets you down or betrays you, look for someone else.

- Always remember it's not your fault. You have a right not to feel like this. You have the right to be listened to.

A SURVIVOR'S STORY

As a child in Ireland, Colm O'Gorman was sexually abused by a priest. When the abuse was happening, he wasn't able to tell anyone. The priest was an important person in his community, and the church was very powerful. At the time, Colm felt completely powerless and blamed himself for what was happening.

In 1984, when Colm was seventeen, he ran away from home and spent some time living on the streets. In time, he began to recover from what had happened, and he decided to report the abuse to the police. He discovered that the same priest had abused lots of other children, and that the church had known he was an abuser.

What Colm discovered led to him campaigning for justice for himself and many other victims of abuse. He campaigned for state investigations and launched legal actions to hold the abuser and the Catholic Church to account. He even sued the Pope. His campaigning helped expose the extent of the cover up of child abuse by the Catholic Church right across the world. Eventually he won his case and, most importantly, an apology from the Church. He is now the director of Amnesty International Ireland.

Colm says of his experiences: 'I am of course proud of what I have achieved as an activist, but what I am happiest about is that I was able to free myself of the shame I took on when I was abused as a child. When I spoke out, lots of people told me that the abuse wasn't my fault. In my head I knew they were right, but I still felt a lot of shame. That's because – despite the fact that I was the victim of this horrible crime and not the perpetrator – that is what abuse does to us, it leaves us feeling bad and shameful. I had lost sight of who I really was and instead all I could see was the abuse. So, I had to allow myself time to work that through, and I got help. If you have been hurt like this it can feel like you are very much alone. But you are not. Ask for help. Find a trusted adult or an organisation in your country that supports young people who have been abused. I promise you that it is possible to get through this, and to find your way back to yourself, to the person you were before this happened and to who you are truly meant to be. The thing I value most is that I found my way back to truly loving myself, and to living a life full of purpose and joy and love. That is what matters more than anything else. You are what matters more than anything else.'

UNDERSTAND YOUR PERSONAL SITUATION

If you want to defend child rights, the first area to explore is the personal. If you need to claim your own rights, you may want to move on to the sections on activism (page 194) and how to navigate the law (page 234). If you want to support others in claiming their rights, read on.

BE CONSCIOUS OF PRIVILEGE

Being aware of privileges, whatever they are, helps us understand difference and why some people don't enjoy the same opportunities as others. It makes it easier to identify and challenge discrimination, which lies at the heart of many abuses of rights all over the world.

Observe your life and those around you. Do you enjoy some rights more or less than other young people? This is a hard process, but be honest with yourself. Do you always treat everyone else with dignity and respect? Are you ever a bully or a bystander, staying silent instead of reporting abuse?

If you saw another child or young person being abused – perhaps verbally or physically – what would

you do? (Consider what you would want them to do if the situation was reversed.) Talk to your peers and friends, and look out for those who are at risk of being badly treated. What would help them? There are many chances to defend human rights, in your home, school or community. Staying silent and being a bystander can allow abuse to flourish. But don't forget about your own well-being and safety: you cannot always take action.

> If you are white, the phrase 'white privilege' doesn't mean that your life isn't hard. It doesn't mean that you haven't experienced denial of your rights. It just means that you are more likely to have experienced benefits and less likely to have suffered discrimination on the basis of your skin colour.

BE A TRANS AND NON-BINARY ALLY

- **Appreciate gender diversity.** If someone is transgender or non-binary, it simply reflects the diversity of human identities.

- **Respect people's names.** Use the name and gender a trans or non-binary person tells you to use. Don't ask what their 'real' name or gender is.

- **Use correct pronouns.** Some people prefer gender-neutral pronouns such as they/their. If you are unsure which pronoun to use, wait for an appropriate moment and ask. Or indicate the pronouns you use first – this gives people an opportunity to say theirs too.

- **Call out transphobia.** Recognise and respect the lives and experiences of all trans and non-binary people, and understand the oppression they face. Challenge friends and family members who make transphobic comments. Dealing with toxic, dehumanising attitudes can be extremely draining and distressing for trans people, so support from others can really help.

- **Listen and learn.** If you make a mistake, apologise and learn from the experience. Honest mistakes don't make you transphobic.

MAKE A CHANGE WHERE YOU LIVE

It is much easier to claim rights and achieve change if public opinion is behind you. Some people start by sharing knowledge at home and in their local community. It is a way to raise awareness which can set off a gradual process of change. So, if you can, discuss rights – or the particular right you are most concerned about – with your family, friends and community. It will help you build awareness and develop circles of influence. People will begin to understand why the right matters, which makes your work easier. Research suggests that hardly anyone changes their minds on something important if they're being shouted at, so, no matter how passionately you care about your cause, try and respect their views. You are more likely to win people over by empathising with their position and reframing your points in a way that is relevant for them.

HOW TO DISCUSS RIGHTS AT HOME

Rights are complex. They can be hard to talk about, perhaps especially with parents or guardians. Here are some steps you could consider.

- If you can, work out in advance what it is you want out of the conversation. It might be as simple as wanting them to listen and understand without offering advice or commentary. Or you might need their permission or support for you to take an action. You might appreciate their advice or help. It's generally helpful to you and them if you tell them what you're looking for at the start of the conversation. (For example, 'I need you to listen without interrupting' or 'I need you to give me some advice'.) Identify your emotions and be as clear as you can about what you think, feel and want.

- Try and pick a time that is convenient for the adult you want to talk to, so they're not stressed or preoccupied.

- Give examples that will help them understand, then they can listen better. Be honest. Try to understand their point of view and, if you can, tell them so, as this is likely to aid good discussion. Speak in a friendly and respectful tone.

- Adults, even parents, won't always see things your way and they won't always say yes to what you ask. It can be hard to take no for an answer, even harder to know that they can't support you. This can happen for a whole host of reasons. If necessary, seek out other trustworthy adults, like a teacher.

COMMON MYTHS AND HOW TO REBUT THEM

There are many arguments made against child rights, and you are likely to face opposition if you try to stand up for them. Here are some especially common myths, with suggestions to help you respond to them.

> 'Children lack experience, you don't know what's in your best interests and you have poor judgement.'

Throughout history people with power have often tried to keep hold of it by saying that others are less competent. This argument was used against women having the vote, for example. Young people with more access to rights will make mistakes, but so do adults. It's no reason for depriving anyone of their full rights.

> 'You don't have the mental capacity to make responsible decisions.'

Wisdom is not measured by age but by a person's maturity or knowledge. Capacity does not simply develop with age. To equate 'capacity' with a moment in time when someone turns eighteen (or the age of majority in your country) is to ignore an enormous group of people on the basis of an arbitrary measure.

> 'You are too easily influenced and can be manipulated by others, so it's dangerous to allow you to participate.'

Everyone is influenced by others to some degree, including adults. Also, if you deny children and young people their rights because they may be manipulated by others, you misunderstand the human rights framework, which is universal and inalienable.

> 'Child rights – like other human rights – are a Western concept and a form of imperialism.'

Every country and culture in the world has communities who experience injustice and discrimination. It is the demands of oppressed people everywhere that led to the growth of human and child rights. Let's not forget that the Convention on the Rights of the Child has been ratified by 196 out of 197 countries.

BUILD A SET OF USEFUL SKILLS

Claiming your rights is made easier if you can clearly articulate your opinions, make a case, raise awareness of the issue and overcome opposition. You might find it helpful to develop skills in these areas.

LEARN TO DEBATE

A debate is a structured argument, where two opposing sides speak for and against an issue. It is a good way to build skills in public speaking and learn how to develop a convincing argument. Many debating groups are modelled on parliamentary systems, so it also helps familiarise you with political language. Debating encourages constructive dialogue. It can change the way you and an audience see an issue.

You could think about joining or starting a debating club. You can put yourself forward to participate in debates and you can also get involved with organising them, perhaps in your community or school.

To prepare for a debate, you need to research your subject and gain good knowledge about it. Think about the topic from all sides, not just your own. You need to foresee what the opposing speaker is likely to say and have your arguments ready. A good start is to write a paper on your chosen topic. If possible, practise with friends.

Here are some tips:

- Speak confidently and clearly.
- Make eye contact with the audience.
- Use strong evidence, facts and powerful language.
- Be alert to the accuracy (or not) of the other speaker's evidence.
- Finish with a strong conclusion – this is often what people remember.
- You can challenge the other speaker, but be respectful.
- Don't worry about being inexperienced, because you will improve with practice.

Model United Nations (MUN) is an activity for young people interested in learning more about how the UN operates. Hundreds of thousands of school and university students worldwide take part every year. You can debate current issues, prepare draft resolutions, plot strategy, negotiate, resolve conflicts, and navigate the UN's rules of procedure. Many of today's leaders in law, government, business and the arts – including at the UN itself – participated in MUN when they were young. If your school doesn't participate in MUN and you are interested, find a teacher who would be willing to help set up an MUN club.

HOW TO MAKE A SPEECH

If you have the chance to speak to an audience, you want to make an impact. Here are some good guidelines.

DO THE PREPARATION:

- The most important thing to work out in advance is your main aim. How do you want your audience to feel? Or what action do you want them to take as a result of your speech? This will affect how you speak to them and what you say.

- Find out about the venue and who your audience will be.

- You don't have to speak the whole time. Plan what action would make sense to achieve your aim. For example, you could show a short video or ask the audience to raise hands.

- Write your speech. Many people read their speeches at the event, but you might prefer to practise it until you know the content very well and can turn it into notes that you can use as prompts. This can help you to sound more natural without forgetting your most important points.

CLAIM YOUR RIGHTS

- Start with something powerful to grab the audience's attention.

- Reveal something about yourself: tell a story, say why this matters to you. The facts you are about to share will be much more meaningful if people have a sense of you as a person.

- Use facts and evidence, but be sure they are relevant and accurate.

- Keep things simple by breaking up complex ideas and issues into manageable parts.

- Use critical thinking and critiquing in a respectful way.

- Consider ending with something positive, a thought that you want the listeners to take away with them.

- Rehearse in front of other people if you can – until the main points flow smoothly while sounding natural.

- Time your speech and make sure it is within your allocated time. People do not usually complain about a short speech and it might give time for audience questions and answers.

- Think about what questions you might be asked so you can prepare answers.

DURING YOUR SPEECH:

- Introduce yourself and say what you are going to talk about and for how long.

- Take your time, breathe, don't rush.

- Look after your audience. Smile. Don't let them get anxious for you.

- Speak slowly. Nearly everyone speaks too fast and it makes it difficult for the audience to absorb what you are saying or for anyone who is translating or signing.

- If you can, speak from your head and heart, but feel free to use your notes as prompts.

- Own the stage. This is a time when you can afford to be a bit bigger than your normal self.

WHEN YOU FINISH:

- Thank your listeners.

- Afterwards, thank the organisers for giving you the opportunity to speak.

- If it didn't go well, don't worry. It gives you something to build on. Each time you speak publicly it is a new experience, a learning opportunity and the chance to present differently to last time.

BECOME AN ACTIVIST

Activism is a route you may want to consider because it can be a powerful way to bring public attention to your cause. It takes many forms. At its heart, it is about taking action and calling for positive change on something that is important to you. It's also about inspiring and supporting others to take action. Even if each action is small, when combined with everyone else's they can have a ripple effect and ultimately achieve a huge impact. Positive change is often credited to politicians or other leaders, but it is nearly always due to long, hard work by dedicated and passionate ordinary people.

Activism is about respecting everyone's equal rights and can be lots of fun. It should not be about self-promotion, being judgemental or denying others their rights. To be a strong activist you need empathy. Be kind. Try and understand different perspectives. Be curious. Uphold other people's right to a voice by listening to them. You can use the knowledge you gain to shape your activist journey. If you are frustrated, remember it's because of systems and individuals that deny rights, not other people like you who are struggling to enjoy their rights.

The following steps are used by many activists:

- You grow a movement around an idea and inspire others to become allies.

- You identify barriers and remove them one by one.

- You find ways to amplify voices so they win over opposition. You use your right to peaceful protest.

- Eventually you increase pressure on the authorities until they have no choice but to act.

This section includes a set of activist tools. However, there are risks in activism and you need to be sure to check the safety guidance carefully. You may have to play your part very quietly, behind the scenes. But remember, *every action matters*. You may succeed in making real change for yourself and others, even if it takes a long time. If not, your activism can still bring hope and inspiration. Remember, small actions create ripples too.

AN ACTIVIST TOOLKIT TO CLAIM YOUR RIGHTS

Activism varies according to your issue and where you are. Do it in a way that works for you, based on your time, your safety and what feels authentic. If possible, discuss with your parents or guardians and keep them in the loop. (See page 185.)

This toolkit includes a range of steps and tactics. They are adaptable. If they are laid out in an order that doesn't suit you, move them around. It's useful to work on them with friends and peers, rather than on your own.

1: IDENTIFY THE PROBLEM	**6: PUT THE PRESSURE ON**
2: DO YOUR RESEARCH	**7: HOLD POLITICIANS TO ACCOUNT**
3: CHOOSE YOUR ALLIES	**8: USE YOUR VOICE INTELLIGENTLY**
4: CREATE A TIMELINE	**9: GO PUBLIC**
5: PLAN A CAMPAIGN	**10: RAISE YOUR VOICE**

1: IDENTIFY THE PROBLEM AND THE CHANGE YOU WANT TO SEE

Identify the rights issue you are passionate about. If you are enjoying a right but others aren't, explore how you can be an ally to them. Your life and experience may be very different to theirs – find out what they want; don't assume their needs and wants are the same as yours.

You need to be clear about your goal and make a plan. Be strategic. Don't dive straight in, no matter how tempting. Ask yourself the questions: Where are we now? Where do we want to go? How are we going to get there?

Look at the problem from all angles. Consider the evidence and the probability of success. This will help you predict different scenarios and outcomes. It will help you shape a strategy: if your first attempt doesn't succeed, you will be ready with a plan B, then a plan C and so on. This will help you persevere.

2: DO YOUR RESEARCH

Research is vital. Find out as many facts as you can before beginning any action. You need to examine the problem, which right is being denied or abused, who is responsible and what needs to change. It will help you clarify how to achieve your goal.

For your research to be worthwhile, accuracy is crucial. Facts matter. Don't accept 'fake news'. Hone your critical questioning skills and work out who to trust as a credible source of information. A good starting point is to think about who might benefit from lying or misleading you and why they might want to spread lies. Don't accept information at face value – always, always check your sources.

Try using these research questions:

- What right is being denied or abused?

- Where is it happening? Is it personal, at home? Is it institutional, embedded in your school, community or place of worship? Is it through a business? Through the police or the government? Is it at national or international level?

- Is there an individual or group of abusers? Who are they?

- What is the law where you live? Political structures are not the same everywhere. This means that laws vary between countries and sometimes in different areas of the same country.

- Who has influence or power to improve the situation? Who are the decision makers? They may be at many different levels.

- Who is misusing their power?

- Who is being a bystander and letting it happen? Rights violations thrive when people either pretend not to see, or turn away.

- What needs to change? What steps would you be happy with?

- What do those in power need to do differently?

- Who could be your allies? Think about individuals, organisations and grassroots groups.

- What would motivate decision makers to pay attention? What pressure could you bring to bear that would encourage them to do the right thing?

3: PEOPLE POWER: CHOOSE YOUR ALLIES

There is real strength in numbers and collective action. Choose allies who care about your cause.

- Start with friends or family members who share your beliefs.

- Think about relevant school groups. You could possibly join or start an Amnesty youth group.

- Research relevant organisations that specialise in your issue. Ask them for advice and support.

- Seek out community groups, networks and grassroots organisations who are interested in your issue. Consider joining them or asking if they would like to work with you.

- Build your own community of other children, young people and supportive adults.

- Remember to encourage diversity. Successful activism thrives on being inclusive, diverse, equitable and accessible. Many movements suffer because people don't feel welcome or included.

- Always be sensitive and open to others' experience, culture and beliefs.

4: CREATE A TIMELINE

To achieve real change you may have to prepare for the long haul, depending on what it is you're fighting for. You might not know the end date: it could be weeks, months, years or even your life's calling.

It will help to put together a timeline of tactics. Include regular activities, such as key dates in your community. Work out when peak moments or opportunities are and schedule activities around them.

Make sure you have the resources and people to make things happen. If you don't, then reduce the scope and aim for something more achievable. Or spread the activities out more so there is a longer gap between them. It will take longer, but it can reduce stress.

5: PLAN A CAMPAIGN

If those in charge are putting obstacles in your path, you could start a campaign and put the spotlight on them. This is very focused activism. You need a clear goal and a timeframe. You can campaign in lots of ways, for example:

- Push for change in government laws or policies.

- Try to influence public attitudes.

- Try to educate the public or key decision makers.

Campaigning can involve public activities and events like **demonstrations** and **marches**, but also behind-the-scenes work like **lobbying** politicians. You will find guidance on these further on in this section.

6: START TO PUT THE PRESSURE ON

Child rights place obligations on leaders. You have the right to use your country's laws to put pressure on those who violate rights and those with the power to improve matters.

Your research will show you which right is being violated or abused, what needs to change and who has the power and influence to make it happen. This may be within your home, school, community, your country or across borders. Remember, you have the right to claim your rights. You are reminding those in power that they are responsible for supporting you and ensuring your rights are upheld.

Consider what change would be enough for you. Depending on what right is being abused, you may feel it is enough for those in charge to:

- Make sure the violation (eg: discrimination) stops.

- Apologise.

- Review their past decisions and actions.

- Change their policy.

- Set up training for those responsible.

- Compensate victims.

But violations that amount to crimes should be investigated and suspects fairly prosecuted, so you may need to follow a more formal legal route. This will vary from setting to setting and you will need to do more research to find out what is appropriate where you live. (See Navigate the law, page 234.)

7: ADVOCACY: HOLD POLITICIANS TO ACCOUNT

It is critical to convince people in power to support you. In many cases, this means politicians, who are ultimately responsible for ensuring rights are upheld. They also have a duty to listen to you, even if you're under eighteen (or the age of majority in your country) or if you're not a citizen of the country where you live. You can hold them to account. The more they hear about what needs changing, the more pressure there is on them to act.

It is possible to succeed without engaging politicians, but it may be harder. Politicians can help you achieve the desired change a lot sooner. Not engaging them can be the difference between failure and success. You can engage them in private or public, depending on what is most effective for you.

This particular activist tool has many parts:

WORK OUT A POLITICAL STRATEGY

First of all, think of your goal and identify which politician(s) are your target. Then work out how best to engage them. Be clear on:

- What is the issue you want addressed?

- Who has the responsibility for the laws, policies or processes related to the issue? Who has the power to create the change? Is it a local, regional or national issue?

- Who are your likely allies in this? A political party? A specific group? Or one or two key politicians?

- What difference can the politician make?

RESEARCH THE POLITICIAN

Next you need to learn about the politician(s) you are seeking to influence. This will help you find a good way to communicate with them. Here are some questions to help.

- What electoral district do you live in? Which politicians represent you at the local, regional or national levels? (Bear in mind that they all have different powers and responsibilities.)

- Which party are they a member of? What are the policies of that party?

- Are they part of the government currently in power? Are they in opposition or an independent?

- Do they have the ability to influence change on your issue?

- What is their position on issues that are important to you? Are they a champion for human or child rights in any way? To find out, you could look up their voting record, social media, or interviews they've given.

- What is their vision? What issues are most important to them? What are they aiming to achieve?

- Who are their allies? Who works with them? Who has influence over them? Which other politicians are they close to? What community groups and organisations are they involved with?

CONTACT YOUR POLITICIAN

It's best to give the politician the chance to respond to you personally before you go public. There are lots of ways to contact them:

- Try to meet them. Keep an eye out for public events they will be attending. This is an opportunity for you to introduce yourself. Be respectful.

- See if your school, college or workplace would invite them in.

- Engage with them on social media. If they see you commenting often, they will start to remember you.

- Write to them. Politicians receive a lot of correspondence, so be sure to say at the beginning that you live in the area they represent, if that is the case.

- Phone their office. Practise what you want to say first. If applicable, identify yourself as a local **constituent**. Leave a message if necessary. Explain why you're calling. Call again, but not too often. Calling after a week or two to ask for an update is reasonable.

- Invite them to attend an event or meeting or other activity. Give them plenty of notice, at least a month.

- Collect petition signatures, perhaps by arranging local activities. A petition (with names and postcodes) is evidence that shows a politician that a lot of their **voters** want change.

You don't have to wait for a possible meeting before working out what your next steps would be. You can be ready ahead of time in case the politician refuses to meet or commit to change. That way you can immediately get into the next phase of your strategy. Next steps can involve going public. It comes down to what will be more effective with that politician, based on what you know about them.

HOW TO WRITE TO A POLITICIAN

You may want to write to a politician to express your concern about a child rights issue. If you are in a country where it is safe to do so, here are some pointers to consider:

Include your name, contact details and the date.

For salutations, see box opposite

Start with the name of the issue or case in capital letters or in bold or underlined, include dates or places where the incidents occurred. For example, 'I am writing to express my concern about . . .'

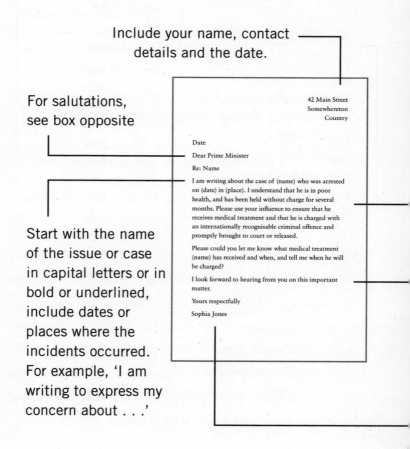

42 Main Street
Somewhereton
Country

Date

Dear Prime Minister

Re: Name

I am writing about the case of (name) who was arrested on (date) in (place). I understand that he is in poor health, and has been held without charge for several months. Please use your influence to ensure that he receives medical treatment and that he is charged with an internationally recognisable criminal offence and promptly brought to court or released.

Please could you let me know what medical treatment (name) has received and when, and tell me when he will be charged?

I look forward to hearing from you on this important matter.

Yours respectfully

Sophia Jones

If you are writing by email, put a clear request in the subject line, so it is seen even if the email is deleted.

Briefly explain the situation and that it is a concern to you. Make your request clearly. For example, 'In order to prevent further abuses, we are asking your government to sign up to the Optional Protocol . . .'

Try to include a phrase that encourages a reply, such as, 'Please confirm what measures you are taking to . . .' or, 'I look forward to hearing from you about what progress . . .'

Sign off respectfully.

How to address officials

Here are some examples to give you an idea.

Monarchs – Your Majesty

Heads of state – Dear President/ Prime Minister, Your Excellency

Ambassadors and High Commissioners – Dear Ambassador or High Commissioner

Local authorities and prison governors – Dear Forename Surname

Judges – Your Honour

Military officials – Dear Admiral/ General/Captain

Members of Parliament in UK/EU – Dear Forename Surname

HOLD AN EFFECTIVE MEETING
WITH YOUR POLITICIAN

If possible, try to meet with your politician as it gives you an opportunity for focused discussion about your cause.

- Identify the member of staff in the politician's office who can help you secure a meeting. Try to build a good relationship with them.

- Send an email or letter to the politician or member of their staff. Include a detailed outline of who you are and what you would like to talk about. Follow this email up with a phone call. You might have to do this more than once. Don't worry if you don't hear from them straightaway or they decline your meeting request. Politicians receive a lot of requests, so persevere.

- The meeting may feel intimidating so prepare for it. Make sure you have support with you. Do not go alone. Between two to four people is ideal. Be sure to coordinate in advance: decide on one person to be the main speaker so as not to confuse your message. You will only have a limited time to talk with the politician, so make sure there are prepared talking points. Have a clear goal, no more than three main requests and discuss the issues in a concise way.

- Remember that you are not expected to be an expert. If the politician asks you a question that you don't know the answer to, tell them you will find that out and get back to them. Make a note of it and follow through with your commitment to find out.

- If you can, point to some possible solutions. They need to hear that there is something practical that they can do to solve the issue. You can let them know what you think the broader government should do, but also what they as an individual can do. That gives them something to progress with after the meeting.

- At the end, thank them for their time and summarise what you are asking for again. If you can, give them a one-page summary of the main points and your three requests, or communicate this in a different way. Make sure they have your contact details so they can follow up on outstanding points.

- Follow up: take notes of the meeting, including the main points discussed and agreed next steps. Read through the notes and think about whether there is something you can improve on next time. Was there an approach that worked well? Was there anything you can share with others in your movement?

- After the meeting, write to the politician (or ask someone who can) and thank them for their time again. Repeat your key points, remind them of what you want and what they agreed to. Make sure you add in any information you said you would find out about. Send them any group pictures you took during your meeting. Let them know that you will keep them up to date about the issues.

There are three possible outcomes:

- The politician agrees with everything and commits to it. This is excellent and all you have to do is follow up with them to make sure they do it.

- The politician agrees to some requests but not everything. You will need to stay in touch and follow up.

- The politician doesn't agree to making the commitment. This is going to mean finding other strategies. At least you know where they stand.

Consider lobbying your politician to investigate child rights violations, especially through special government committees. You could encourage them to set up dedicated child rights committees. If not, press them to ensure that other human rights committees give plenty of attention to child rights.

8: USE YOUR VOICE INTELLIGENTLY

To achieve change, how you communicate is crucial. You need to inspire people to join you, not make them turn away. This takes careful planning as well as creativity.

First, identity the target audience. Who do you want to reach? How are you going to get your message to them? Knowing your target audience helps you work out how to inspire them. Be clear about who you are targeting and try to understand the context of their lives. Get to know their concerns and motivations. What would grab their attention in a positive way?

Then work out how to get them on your side:

- Be clear about your campaign, who you are and what your goal is.

- Try to make the issue personal – use stories of real people to make it clear what you are talking about and show the potential impact.

- Make sure that you get others' full consent before you use their photos or stories.

- Use hopeful messaging to inspire people to believe they can make a difference.

- Avoid words or images that might trigger fear or trauma.

- Clearly explain which right is being violated and why it matters.

- Say who is responsible for denying the right.

- Use clear, simple and active words.

- Use words and pictures that respect others' rights and that are inclusive.

- Be clear what you want people to do.

Consider going into politics. You could be a future leader and decision maker who takes a rights-respecting approach. A good route is to start small and local, such as joining a school student council, so you can hone your skills and develop your understanding of the political process. Watch politicians and see how they do it. Engage directly with them and ask for their advice.

9: GO PUBLIC

You might want to launch a public campaign. If a significant section of the public supports your goals, it can put pressure on people in power to take action.

You may need to be persistent and show that your campaign will carry on until the change happens.

Again, be strategic. Identify your key audience. Look at what – and who – you have to support you and work out what is likely to have the biggest impact. Remember to look after your safety and that of others at all times.

Here are some steps you could consider:

BUILD AWARENESS

Adapt your voice. Firstly, use the research you have done on the politician or other 'campaign targets' (someone else who has power to make change on your issue). Think about how best to influence them. We all change our way of communicating depending on who we're talking to – for example, you probably speak to your best friend in a different way to your teacher. The same applies when campaigning.

Think about how you can engage large numbers of the public, or people in your community. Do some research about who you're trying to get on board and how to do it best. Tell them the story of what you care about and how your passion was born. This will encourage others to join you.

Get your message out there in creative and innovative ways. Talk to the media – it could be local, national or international media. Engage on social media. Hold your own community events or set up a stall at one. Stick posters up.

Think creatively. What sort of action might draw the attention (and support) of the general public, the media *and* your campaign target? Art installations, silent protests, creative messages on banners and forms of 'non-violent direct action' can be great ways of engaging people in a memorable way.

Non-violent direct action covers a range of activities, from letter writing and collecting petition signatures, to rallies, demonstrations and media stunts. Examples include hosting a vigil outside an embassy, holding or participating in a rally, writing chalk slogans on the ground, or media stunts. Only do these if it is safe where you live.

Once you've built awareness on your issue, encourage members of the community to get involved in your activism. They might be willing to sign petitions or join a peaceful protest, for example. Try to think of any community leaders, organisations or people who may have influence over your campaign target. See if they will contact and discuss the matter with the target.

AMPLIFY YOUR CAMPAIGN

If you can, create or devote one or more social media accounts for your campaign work. Follow other activists and influencers whose interests and values are relevant to your campaign objectives, join their conversations and try to engage them in yours. Building sympathetic networks with shared purpose online is a great way to reach wider audiences and can help you amplify your campaign actions.

Being outspoken on social media, however, can attract unwanted attention. Be mindful of whether it's safe to put your face to the campaign. Ignore trolls and be

very vigilant about anyone who asks to meet in person. Never meet anyone new alone, always go as part of a group, unless you are in a very safe public setting. Always use passwords to protect your work.

Research influencers or people in the public eye who have spoken out or shown support for the rights you are trying to claim. You can try to engage with them online. Remember that high-profile individuals with millions of followers are less likely to respond, but that doesn't mean you shouldn't try. Consider people with smaller platforms who write their own posts, engage with their followers and are vocal about social change. If they amplify your messages or calls to action, it will have more impact because it will feel authentic to their followers who, in turn, may support your campaign.

KEEP ENGAGING WITH THE POLITICIAN

Find ways to keep engaging with the campaign target. If you are able and it is safe, you could follow them online, go to events they will be attending and keep asking questions. You could also engage politely and constructively with their social media posts. If needed, keep asking for meetings or a change to their response. Make sure that they don't forget you are around and what you want from them.

> Take care! Think carefully about any risks that might arise from your campaign. Putting your face to a public campaign can potentially bring harassment and violence in person or online. Depending on where you live in the world, it can be very dangerous. Before you do anything, think about all the possible scenarios or consequences, including negative things. How can you plan ahead to minimise those risks?

10: RAISE YOUR VOICE: USE YOUR RIGHT TO PEACEFUL PROTEST

As well as freedom of expression, you have the right to peaceful protest. You can assemble – this means meet with others – for a common cause. It is your right to be creatively defiant to bring about positive change.

Use your voice safely and intelligently and be very clear about which rights you are claiming.

You and your friends are bound to have plenty of different talents at your disposal. Be spectacular, disrupt the status quo, agitate peacefully and grab people's attention. Whether your techniques are online or offline – on social media or making giant street puppets for a march – try to bring attention to your cause.

The more you succeed in getting publicity, the more you will raise public awareness for your cause. If you provoke awareness and thoughtfulness, you are more likely to contribute to positive change.

Protest is a powerful tool. Providing it's safe, know that you have the right to claim your rights. Assert your rights, have fun and be confident.

ORGANISING A PROTEST MARCH OR DEMONSTRATION

Depending on where you live, there will be rules and regulations. You may have to give the police written notice of your plans, the date, time and your intended route but you don't need their permission. They may ask you to change this for logistical reasons, but they all have a legal duty to help a peaceful protest take place within 'sight and sound' of the intended target. Check and comply with your country's regulations in advance.

KNOW YOUR RIGHTS ON PROTEST MARCHES

Despite the fact that it's a human right, protest marches often provoke violent responses from the state, especially the police. You need to take great care for your safety and know your rights:

- Everyone has the right to carry their opinion onto the streets.

- The right to protest peacefully should be facilitated by police and law enforcement agencies, not restricted by them dispersing the protest or arresting or intimidating you.

- You still have a right to protest peacefully, even if a few individuals are protesting violently.

Police officers should not use the violent acts of a few as reason to disperse the protest or take action against peaceful protesters. Police are there to serve you, not intimidate you. They should always try to calm things down before the situation worsens.

- In all countries, police officers should be responsible for upholding the law and protecting the rights of all members of society, not picking and choosing who they want to protect and who they do not.

- Guns should never be used against you by the authorities for the purpose of dispersing the crowd.

- You have a right to medical assistance, without any delays.

- You have a right to document the protest – the authorities should not keep you from filming or writing down what police actions, police violence, or injuries are inflicted on protestors.

Only in exceptional cases can a protest be dispersed – for example, if there is clear evidence of a threat of serious violence – and when less intrusive measures, such as targeted arrests, are not enough. You have the right to be safe from rubber bullets, tear gas, and stun grenades. They can result in serious injury and death and, therefore, according to international standards, these weapons can only be used to disperse a protest as an exceptional measure of last resort. Their use

Packing for a protest

Warning: be aware of your context. In some countries police search protestors. They may arrest you if you are carrying something that they interpret as a predictor of violence. If tear gas is likely it is safest not to attend. See page 226.

In a small bag or backpack take water, snacks, hand sanitiser, a face mask if necessary, sunscreen, a warm layer and/or rainwear if appropriate, and some cash.

Bring your fully charged phone if you have one – but check your digital security (see page 230).

Write down an emergency contact number on your hand or piece of paper in case your phone runs out of battery.

Wear comfortable clothing and shoes so you can be out for a long time and run if necessary.

Get creative and make a placard – maybe check it with a friend to make sure your message can be understood.

must conform to the principles of legality, necessity and proportionality – this means that their use is governed by national laws, is necessary to achieve a legitimate aim (such as protecting life) and is the least intrusive or restrictive way to achieve that aim. The UN has published online basic principles of the use of force and firearms by law enforcement officials, which you can look up if you have Internet access.

KEEP YOURSELF SAFE ON PROTEST MARCHES

- Consider not attending if the risks are great. Think about how the authorities in your country usually react to protests. In some countries the response can be violent, even deadly.

- Follow any relevant healthcare advice, such as wearing a face mask. If you are unwell or at risk, don't go.

- Be aware that security forces can mis-identify cameras and filming equipment as a threat.

- Stay alert to the situation, no matter what type of protest or vigil it is. The tone or mood can change quickly, as can the response from police.

- If possible, don't go to a protest on your own. Try to protest with a group of people. Have a pre-arranged 'safe zone' or meeting point where you and your friends can meet if separated.

- When you get to a protest, always check where police are located and where your nearest exit is from that location.

- Be constantly aware of what is happening around you. If you don't feel comfortable, remove yourself from the situation. If something happens and tensions rise, try to stay calm and focused and react to danger or warning signs sooner rather than later.

- Ignore verbal bait from passers-by or counter-protesters. Don't get into unnecessary arguments.

- If you are caught in a fleeing crowd, try to identify ways to escape that are off to the side and away from the flow of traffic. Plan an escape route in advance.

- If you are from a minority group, in some countries you may be at more risk of police violence. If you are part of the majority group, whoever that is in your country, be alert to who needs allies and show your solidarity.

What to do if you encounter tear gas and pepper spray

If you see it coming and notice police are putting gas masks on, try to escape and get upwind. If you have any, put on protective gear such as shatterproof swimming goggles. Warning: carrying these items could put you at risk from the authorities in some countries.

Stay calm. Panicking increases the irritation.

Breathe slowly and remember it is only temporary.

Blow your nose, rinse your mouth, cough and spit. Try not to swallow.

If you wear contact lenses, remove them or get someone to do it for you, with clean, uncontaminated fingers. Destroy the lenses after exposure, they are not cleanable. The most important aspect is not to rub it in. Carry a spare pair of glasses as a back-up.

Use an eye flush with a solution of half liquid antacid and half water. This only applies to aluminium hydroxide or magnesium hydroxide-based antacids such as Maalox, not simethicone-based antacids. Remember to take water with you. Warning: carrying an eye flush could put you at risk from the authorities in some countries.

As soon as possible after dealing with immediate medical concerns, walk around with your arms outstretched, remove contaminated clothing and take a cool shower.

WHAT TO DO IF YOU'RE STOPPED BY THE POLICE

If you are stopped by the police, your response can help to reduce the risk of your rights being violated.

Educate yourself in advance

Some countries offer special guidelines for police conduct towards under-eighteens. Ideally you should research and learn the rules that apply in your country (or the country you are in), so that you know what your rights are if you are stopped by the police.

To reduce the risk of police misconduct, you can ask the police what law they are relying on to stop, question or search you. But be mindful of the policing culture in your country and how the police are likely to respond if you challenge them or refuse to comply with unlawful requests. There are potential risks in standing up for your rights. Your safety comes first.

How to talk to the police

- Stay calm – talk to the police respectfully, do not try to evade or obstruct them, and do not express hostility or aggression.

- Only provide your name or identification to the police if there is a legal requirement to do so.

- In many countries, you have the right to remain silent. Learn the law in your country, avoid giving the police false information and do not answer questions unless there is a legal requirement to do so.

- In some countries the police can only search you and your belongings if they have reasonable suspicion that you are concealing illegal or stolen items. In others they can only search you if they have a warrant. Learn about the search procedures in your country and do not consent to unlawful searches.

If you are arrested

If the police arrest and take you into custody, you should immediately request a solicitor or lawyer and do not answer any questions, sign anything or make decisions without talking confidentially to your solicitor.

How to make a complaint

Even if you do everything possible to reduce the risk, the police may still violate your rights. You may be able to file a legal complaint. Here are some steps you can take:

- During any interaction with a police officer, try to take a note of their name, badge number and the station or division they belong to. These details could be important later if you need to make a complaint.

- If it is safe, you or a bystander can record a video of your interaction with the police which could be used as evidence if your rights are violated.

- Speak to potential witnesses and take their names and details if possible.

- As evidence, take photographs of any injuries you may have sustained and seek immediate medical attention.

UNDERSTAND DIGITAL SECURITY

In some countries governments are known or believed to use secret surveillance techniques, including 'spyware' to monitor human rights activists. This violates privacy rights and the acceptable limits of state surveillance.

Try to educate yourself about the risks, based on laws and practices in your country, and being mindful that you may also encounter false conspiracy theories. If you have any devices like a phone, check the advice here. Understanding digital security and best practices helps improve your readiness for a protest. It also helps you, your friends and community stay safe.

If you are planning to join a protest, a phone can be a vital tool. You depend on it to access information, organise with your peers, document events and help others.

Here are some practical tips for mobile phone safety before joining a protest.

Possible risks with using a mobile phone at a protest:

■ Losing your phone.

■ Police confiscating your device.

■ Service disruption due to mobile network failures and overload.

Surveillance risks in some countries:

■ Installing malicious spyware onto activists' phones.

■ Monitoring communications over radio services such as walkie-talkies and other comms over radio.

■ Interfering with web services, such as throttling access to popular social media sites like Twitter.

■ Disrupting messaging and voice services such as Signal or WhatsApp.

■ Targeting public wi-fi near the protest to monitor traffic and identify connected devices.

■ Retrieving records from cell towers near a protest to track and identify people.

Before joining a protest it's a good idea to:

■ Make sure your phone has screen lock enabled. Use at least a 6-digit PIN code, or preferably a passphrase. If you use biometric unlock, such as fingerprint or face ID, be mindful that it might be used to forcibly unlock your phone. You might want to disable those options.

- Back up your phone: make sure to back up all content, including contacts, texts, media and any other personal content. Remember to back up your messaging apps too.

- Pack a spare mobile battery or fully charged power bank.

- Write down on a piece of paper, or even on yourself with a marker, important information such as an emergency contact or a lawyer's number.

- Top up your mobile phone credit and make sure you have enough data allowance.

- Familiarise yourself with the apps you plan to use at the protest and make sure all apps are up to date.

- Check your phone's storage: you don't want your phone to run out of storage suddenly so make sure you have enough space and/or use an external SD card.

- Set up device shortcuts: you can be more discreet while using your phone in public and save time by knowing buttons and keyboard shortcuts. For example, use a shortcut to turn on the camera or to send an emergency message. Learn and practise these shortcuts; you might be able to customise them.

- Consider setting up the 'Find Your Phone' function so you can locate and wipe your phone remotely if you need to. Most smartphones provide a method to do this. Make sure you are familiar with it.

Using the phone's camera:

- When at the protest, little things could draw unnecessary attention, such as the camera flash or shutter sound. Go through your camera settings and configure it for safe use.

- Your phone could get snatched while filming, so remember to open the camera from the locked screen shortcut instead of unlocking your phone. If your phone is taken, they won't have access to your media or phone's content.

- Be mindful of others' privacy. While capturing photos and videos, the identity of your friends and peers could be at risk of being exposed. Obscure their identities in pictures before sharing them. You can use the quick editor on your mobile media app, and explore apps that help, such as ObscuraCam for Android, and for iPhone use the blur tools with Signal app to preserve privacy.

At the protest:

- To communicate with your peers before and during a protest try using apps that provide end-to-end encryption, such as Signal or Wire.

- Authorities might use tactical equipment, such as rogue cell towers, or request data from mobile operators in order to identify protesters. When you are not making calls or accessing Internet services, you might want to set the smartphone in airplane mode in order to block transmissions and minimise tracking. This also helps save battery life.

NAVIGATE THE LAW

Depending on which right concerns you most, you may want to seek a change in the laws in your country. As you know, all governments who have ratified the Convention on the Rights of the Child – and other human rights treaties – have made a promise under international law. They have a legal obligation not just to keep their promise but to implement it in their country. The question is, are they doing it effectively or does something need to change?

The Convention asks governments to comply 'in good faith'. It doesn't say exactly how they should implement child rights because political structures are so different. This means that there is quite a variety of ways in which different countries (and states) implement child rights through their laws. Legal processes vary too, which can make it very tricky to work out how to claim them. It also makes it impossible to give clear legal guidance that is the same across the world. You will need to research what applies where you live and you will probably feel as if you have entered a legal maze. Try talking to a local law office, charity or NGO to see if they have any useful resources, or to a lawyer or teacher to find out more detail. It is also worth knowing that the more young people who come together to claim rights, the more likely it is you will succeed. Solidarity and collective action can be very effective.

> If you live in the United States, which hasn't ratified the Convention, you still have routes to claim your rights. The US is a federal system, so local states can include child rights in their state constitution. States and provinces can also initiate state or provincial laws that include children's rights, even if the state itself cannot incorporate the Convention, which would have to be at national level. You could also consider joining a campaign for the US to ratify the Convention.

DIFFERENT WAYS FOR GOVERNMENTS TO IMPLEMENT CHILD RIGHTS

Governments are made up of people. Like most of us, they may be tempted to follow the simplest or cheapest paths. They may pick and choose the protections that are easiest for them to implement.

If your country has 'directly incorporated' the Convention into its domestic law, this is good. It means that the Convention is integrated into all legislation concerning children. It is binding on public agencies and can be enforced in court.

But if your country uses what is called 'indirect incorporation', there is little enforcement power for child rights. It needs fuller laws by government to make the Convention fully effective. A third approach is called a 'piecemeal or sectoral approach', whereby some governments cherry-pick which of your rights to include in national law and which to ignore. Clearly this can lead to abuses.

There is also the issue of governments who have applied reservations to particular rights, so they don't fully uphold them (see page 24). You can research if your government is one of them. If it is, and if you don't agree with it, you can campaign for the reservation to be withdrawn.

You could also consider campaigning for your country to directly incorporate the Convention into domestic law, which makes a big difference to child rights. Research who else is already campaigning on this and how to add your voice.

WHO IS IN CHARGE OF CHILD RIGHTS?
NATIONALLY

Your government is supposed to ensure that your rights are protected in every aspect of your life. Politicians are responsible for the smooth running of a country, as well as how laws are implemented. This includes at local, regional and national level.

Public agencies that are regulated by government, like law courts, police, schools, social services and hospitals, have an obligation to uphold child rights.

If you want to change local laws, you have a range of campaigning options, depending on the nature of your local government. For example, where local authorities have less law-making power, you could call for a local law (also called an ordinance) that requires all local

officials to abide by everything in the Convention. You could also ask for all judges and lawyers to be trained in child rights.

If your rights are violated or abused, you can go to the people who work in the relevant organisation and also appeal to politicians. They are obliged to try and resolve it for you. So, if you are discriminated against in school, for example, you can take your complaint up the chain of command, from your teacher to your head teacher, the school board, the local authority, your local politician and your country's Ministry for Education, through law courts if necessary.

If your ultimate goal is to change the law in your country, you will find it very challenging. Laws are often intricately linked with public opinion and traditions, so you may need to embark on long-term education and awareness-raising.

You could consider pushing for dedicated child rights commissioners or **ombudspersons** in your state or country. Their role is to give more focused attention and protection to child rights.

TAKING ACTION

Climate activist Marinel Sumook Ubaldo was sixteen when she experienced the devastating impact of climate change. On 13 November 2013, Typhoon Yolanda, one of the most powerful on record, destroyed her village, Matarinao, in Eastern Samar province in the Philippines. The typhoon killed 6,300 people and millions lost their homes. People were relocated to sites without basic services such as water and electricity. There were few opportunities to earn a living. Many returned to their original homes, even though they were in dangerous areas.

Marinel said that the government's response was inadequate and she became a leading youth activist. She pushed the Philippines government to meet the needs of the people of Matarinao. She also asked the Philippines Commission on Human Rights to investigate forty-seven major fossil fuel and carbon-producing companies for human rights violations linked to climate impacts. It was the first time ever that a country's human rights commission investigated corporate responsibility for climate change. It may set the foundations for future legal action against companies responsible for climate change.

HOW TO TAKE LEGAL ACTION

If you have already tried contacting your politician (see page 206) and they are unwilling to support you, you can look into taking legal action yourself. Here are some useful steps:

- First, find out what the procedures are where you live or in the place where you want to take action.

- If it is possible and appropriate, discuss with your family whether they agree it's a good idea to take a more formal legal route.

- See if you can find a human rights or child rights lawyer who will advise you *pro bono* (for free) – many countries have them.

- You can also research if your country offers legal aid, which is free legal support for people who can't afford to pay.

- In some countries, civil society organisations or groups will take legal action on your behalf. This may be a safer way to proceed because you do not have to be identified to the public.

- Choose a lawyer who takes you seriously and whom you can trust.

- Ensure the lawyer will protect your and others' safety.

- Do not begin legal action unless it is safe for you to do so.

INTERNATIONALLY

On a global level, each of the core international human rights treaties has a treaty body, which is a committee of independent experts who monitor how well those rights are upheld in countries around the world. The treaty body for the Convention is the UN Committee on the Rights of the Child. All governments who have ratified the Convention have to provide regular country reports. The Committee scrutinises what countries are doing with regards to child rights and is alert to violations. If a country breaks the law, it faces a set of possible consequences depending on the gravity of the offence.

Sometimes the Committee, like the other UN treaty bodies, publishes General Comments. These are documents with guidelines for governments who have ratified a treaty. They help clarify and interpret specific concerns. They may outline potential violations and offer advice on how governments should comply with their obligations.

The Committee also oversees Optional Protocol 3 (OP 3, see page 31). If you are battling to have your rights upheld, have tried all the normal legal procedures in your country and are still struggling, look to see if your country has ratified OP 3. If it has, you can take your complaint to the Committee. If it hasn't, you may be able to use another UN mechanism or a human rights treaty body in your region. They are the African Charter, the European Convention on Human Rights, the European Social Charter, the Inter-American Convention on Human Rights and the Inter-American Protocol of San Salvador. However, some countries do not belong to any of these regional treaty bodies, nor have they ratified Optional Protocol 3. You may want to look into campaigning for them to do so.

TAKING ACTION

In September 2019, sixteen climate activists aged eight to seventeen petitioned the UN Committee on the Rights of the Child. The activists included: Chiara Sacchi (Argentina), Catarina Lorenzo (Brazil), Iris Duquesne (France), Raina Ivanova (Germany), Ridhima Pandey (India), Litokne Kabua, David Ackley

III and Ranton Anjain (Marshall Islands), Deborah Adegbile (Nigeria), Carlos Manuel (Palau), Ayakha Melithafa (South Africa), Greta Thunberg (Sweden), Raslene Joubal (Tunisia), Alexandria Villasenor and Carl Smith (United States). They presented a landmark official complaint to protest lack of government action on the climate crisis and said that UN Member States' failure to tackle the climate crisis is a violation of child rights. They urged the Committee to order governments to take action to protect children from the devastating impacts of climate change. They filed their complaint using Optional Protocol 3.

> We all have the right to enjoy our planet and we should all protect that right. Our generation is trying to prevent climate change for future generations.'

Carlos Manuel

LOOK AFTER YOUR MENTAL HEALTH

Activism and claiming your rights can be fun and empowering. You are working with others who have the same dreams and the same drive as you, who want to protect and respect human rights around the world.

But activism is something you do, not who you are. It can be crucial to separate the two, because there's another side to activism. While you're trying to make the world a better place, you see the worst of it. It can make you question what you're doing, and why. It can make you ask, 'What's the point?' And it can affect your mental health.

Activism and volunteering can be very stressful. Stress is how your mind and body react to demands or threats. It happens when there is a build-up of pressure that is above what you can tolerate. Sometimes being under pressure is not necessarily a bad thing, but in the long-term it can become chronic and negatively affect your overall physical and emotional health.

Feeling stressed does not mean you are weak, it is completely normal. Recognising and understanding the signs and causes can help you address them and deal with them. Here are some common stress factors for activists:

- Taking on too much and feeling guilty for taking a break.

- Unhealthy boundaries: you start overlooking your own well-being and that of others.

- Young activists report feeling very stressed in environments that are centred around adults.

- Global socio-political and environmental affairs: following the news can itself feel stressful at times.

BURNOUT

If you sometimes feel guilty, overwhelmed, demotivated, cynical or emotionally drained and detached, you may be facing **burnout**. Burnout is a condition of exhaustion and disconnection that develops gradually within a chronic stressful environment. It can have serious consequences, such as anxiety, reduced performance, insomnia, social withdrawal, attention impairment, negative thoughts and life dissatisfaction. Experts recognise that activist and volunteer burnout is one of the biggest barriers to sustaining social justice movements. In the long run it can actually hinder social change.

SELF-CARE AND RESILIENCE

What is self-care? And how can you stay combative, resilient and motivated given the current state of the world?

Self-care can be:

- Listening to your body – really listening – and getting enough sleep, moving and exercising, eating a nutritious diet and doing what feels good to you.

- Taking digital breaks. In this super-connected world, it feels hard to disconnect. Take a day to recharge; draw, sing, read, write, dance, visit a friend, go to your local park or do nothing. Remember: you have the right to play and relax, so make the most of it.

- Feeling proud of what you are doing.

- Taking time to create safe places and moments for you and others in your community where you take care of each other. This can include opportunities to talk about difficult issues or good ways to relax.

- Putting up some healthy boundaries. You may feel the need to get involved in everything, particularly when a certain issue seems urgent. If you feel you have too much on your plate, or need to rest, you should say NO.

- Practising mindfulness and meditation: take some time on a daily basis to unwind.

PART FOUR

RESOURCES AND OTHER INFORMATION

4

RESOURCES

You've read the book and are now equipped with knowledge about your rights. You may need to do some more research in order to claim them, and we hope this last section will be helpful. It includes a list of useful terms as well as some organisations that work on child rights and who may be able to provide you with further information and support. We also list the organisations whose invaluable work we drew on in compiling this book. You'll see how we approached the creation of this radical book and who helped us.

USEFUL TERMS

ABUSE Wrongful treatment that goes against human rights, carried out by individuals and companies. 'Abuser' is also used for someone who tries to control their victim in an intimate or sexual way.

ACTIVISM Taking action and calling for positive change on something that is important to you.

AGE OF MAJORITY The age at which you legally become an adult, with the rights and responsibilities of adulthood.

AGENCY Your capacity to act independently and make your own choices.

ANTI-RACISM To act in ways that uphold racial equality and the need for equal treatment, and that combat racism.

ANTI-SEMITISM Prejudice against or hatred of Jewish people.

ARTICLE A clause within a treaty. In the Convention on the Rights of the Child, the 54 Articles lay out your rights, a set of rules for governments and the procedures of the Committee on the Rights of the Child.

ASYLUM SEEKER Someone who has left their country because of persecution and serious human rights violations, but who hasn't yet been legally recognised as a refugee and is waiting to receive a decision on their asylum claim in another country. Seeking asylum is a human right.

BURNOUT A condition of exhaustion and disconnection that develops within a chronic stressful environment.

CASTE A hereditary form of social hierarchy that gives privileges to some and discriminates against others.

CENSORSHIP The control and suppression of words, images, ideas and media that the authorities consider unacceptable.

CHARTER A formal document that defines the functions and lays down the rules of an organisation; or a legal agreement that grants rights from one body to another.

CHILD RIGHTS Human rights belonging to all children from the moment of birth until the age of majority.

CIVIL SOCIETY A loose term referring to a space where there is collective action around shared interests and goals. Usually distinct from government and commercial for-profit companies, civil society includes charities, non-governmental organisations, community groups, women's and faith-based organisations, trade unions and other types of groups.

CLIMATE CRISIS The devastating environmental consequences of climate change and global warming, largely man-made and caused by burning fossil fuels for energy and transport, cutting down forests and poor agricultural practices. Effects include rising sea levels, dying coral reefs, mass extinctions of wildlife, natural disasters, weather extremes, food and water insecurity, economic disruption, conflict, and terrorism.

COLONIALISM When a power sets up colonies or settlements in other countries for the political and economic benefit of the colonising country. It is underpinned by imperialism.

COMMITTEE ON THE RIGHTS OF THE CHILD A body of 18 independent child rights experts who regularly monitor how well governments are putting child rights into practice in their countries.

COMPREHENSIVE SEXUALITY EDUCATION (CSE) An age-appropriate, culturally relevant approach to teaching about sex and relationships by providing scientifically accurate, realistic and non-judgemental information.

CONCENTRATION CAMP A place where people are imprisoned without a trial and treated in a cruel, inhuman and degrading way. In Nazi-controlled Europe, there was a network of concentration camps built to mass murder Jewish people and other groups, or to use them as slave labour.

CONSCRIPTION When you are made to join an armed force.

CONSENT In sexual relationships, this means that you are able to communicate clearly, say whether or not you wish to participate and be taken seriously. It includes being aware and respectful of boundaries.

CONSTITUENT In a democracy, you are the constituent of a politician who represents the area (or constituency) where you live.

CONVENTION A legally binding agreement between states or countries. Governments that ratify a convention have a legal obligation to uphold it.

CORPORAL PUNISHMENT Any punishment, including smacking, in which physical force is used and intended to cause some degree of pain or discomfort.

CRIMES AGAINST HUMANITY Includes crimes like murder, rape and persecution committed as part of a planned widespread and systematic attack against a civilian population.

CYBERBULLYING Any form of bullying that happens online or through smartphones or tablets.

DEBT BONDAGE A form of child slavery when children are forced into work to pay off a debt owed by them or their families.

DEMOCRACY When the citizens of a state or country vote to choose their political representatives and their government.

DEMONSTRATION When groups of people organise to come together at a specific place and time in order to call attention to a particular issue.

DEPRIVATION OF LIBERTY Arrest, detention or imprisonment including in prisons, institutions, immigration centres and other places of control.

DIRECT/DOMESTIC INCORPORATION When a government upholds child rights by embedding the Convention on the Rights of the Child into its country's laws.

DISCRIMINATION Treating someone unfairly because of who they are – for example, due to their race, gender, gender identity, religion, culture, sexuality, disability, wealth or poverty.

EARLY FORCED MARRIAGE Also known as child marriage, this is when marriage is forced on a child under the age of eighteen, often a girl made to marry a much older man. It is a form of sexual violence because the girls are not able to give consent.

ETHNIC CLEANSING The deliberate mass killings of people on the basis of their ethnic group.

ETHNICITY The shared cultural heritage of a group, including aspects such as language and religion.

EVOLVING CAPACITIES The rates at which children develop and mature, gradually gaining autonomy because you are increasingly able to take on responsibility. It varies according to children's environments, cultures, life experiences and capabilities.

FEMALE GENITAL MUTILATION (FGM) Also known as cutting, this is a violent procedure performed on girls, partly or entirely removing or damaging the female genitals in order to inhibit girls' and women's sexual feelings and restrict or remove their ability to feel intimate pleasure.

FORCED LABOUR Work done against your will and under the threat of punishment, from which you can't easily escape.

GENDER-BASED VIOLENCE (GBV) Any harmful act perpetrated against someone because of socially ascribed gender differences. It includes sexual violence, intimate partner violence (also called domestic violence), forced and early marriage and FGM.

GENDER BINARY The idea that there are only two genders, male and female, because binary means 'having two parts'.

GENDER DYSPHORIA Emotional distress caused by the conflict between someone's gender assigned by society and the gender with which they identify.

GENDER STEREOTYPING Persistent attitudes that encourage boys and men to dominate, which limit everyone's thinking and choices, and restrict girls' and women's lives.

GENERAL COMMENTS Documents published by UN human rights treaty monitoring bodies that give guidance to governments who have ratified a treaty. They help clarify and interpret concerns. Sometimes they outline potential violations and offer advice to governments on how to comply with their obligations.

GENOCIDE The deliberate murder of as many people as possible belonging to a national, ethnic, racial or religious group.

HATE CRIME Criminal behaviour motivated by prejudice and hostility towards someone else on the basis of disability, race, religion, sexual orientation or gender identity.

HOLOCAUST The deliberate murder by the Nazis of 6 million Jewish people, as well as other minorities, in World War Two.

HOMOPHOBIA Discrimination against LGBT people because of their sexuality.

HUMAN RIGHTS International laws that are rooted in values such as equality, freedom, dignity and justice, designed to protect everyone from oppression and abuse of power.

IMPERIALISM A country's policy to influence or take over other countries or territories through military force and other means of power. Imperialism is the set of ideas that leads to colonialism.

IMPUNITY When those who have committed human rights violations are not brought to justice.

INALIENABLE When this is said of human rights, it means that no one can take them away.

INDIGENOUS PEOPLE People who are native to a region or territory, with distinct practices and traditions away from mainstream society and culture.

INTERNALLY DISPLACED When you are forced out of your home by violence and conflict, but you remain in your country.

ISLAMOPHOBIA Prejudice against or hatred of Muslim people.

LEGALLY BINDING Signatories are legally obliged to keep to the agreement (or contract), which can be enforced by law.

LGBTI Lesbian, gay, bisexual, transgender and intersex.

LOBBYING When you try to influence the decisions and actions of politicians and government.

MARCH A form of demonstration when people come together and march along an agreed route, using the right to peaceful protest and assembly.

MIGRANT Someone who leaves or flees their home to go to new places – usually abroad – to seek a better or safer future. Many migrants do not fit the legal definition of a refugee but could nevertheless be in danger if they went home. Those who have not fled persecution are still entitled to all human rights.

MINORITY GROUP People whose ethnicity, race, language or religion are different to those of the dominant group in their country.

NEURODIVERSE Refers to the multiple ways in which the human brain functions, learns and processes information. People with autism, dyslexia, dyspraxia or bipolar disorder, for example, may be termed neurodiverse and usually face additional social obstacles.

NEUROTYPICAL When the brain functions and processes information in the way that society expects.

NON-BINARY GENDER Used to describe people who do not experience themselves as either male or female, so do not fall within the gender binary.

NON-STATE ENTITIES/ACTORS Any entity that is not actually a state, often used to refer to armed groups, civil society, religious groups or business corporations.

NON-VIOLENT DIRECT ACTION Methods of protest where the intention is to disrupt without causing physical or personal damage.

OMBUDSPERSON A public official who investigates complaints and acts as an impartial intermediary to help resolve disputes. This scheme exists in some countries only.

OPPRESSION The cruel or unjust exercise of power over less-privileged individuals or groups.

OPTIONAL PROTOCOL A treaty that complements and adds to an existing human rights treaty.

PEOPLE OF COLOUR People who self-identify or are perceived as Black or Brown, a term often used within a white majority environment.

PERIOD POVERTY Being unable to afford sanitary products and clean, safe spaces in which to use them, which holds back many girls from accessing education and other rights.

PERPETRATOR The person, organisation, government or non-state actor who has committed abuses or violations of rights.

POST-TRAUMATIC STRESS An anxiety disorder caused by very stressful, frightening or distressing events.

PRIVILEGE Having incidental benefits that come from belonging to a specific social group or because of your identity (your gender or race, for example).

RACISM Racial discrimination.

RATIFY To sign and agree to be legally bound by a treaty.

REFUGEE Someone who has fled their own country because they are at risk of serious human rights violations and persecution if they stay there. Refugees have a right to international protection.

RESERVATIONS TO TREATIES When a government that ratifies a treaty declares it may not abide by one or more clauses in the treaty. It is a means for governments not to uphold some rights fully.

SCAPEGOATING Blaming people or groups for social problems undeservedly, often to divert attention from the real cause.

SLAVERY A system where people treat others as their property to control and exploit them, often for financial gain.

SOLIDARITY A shared sense of humanity that enables you to connect with and support other people, no matter your differences.

STATE The political organisation of a society, usually used to refer to local and national government.

SURVEILLANCE A form of monitoring, often of your communications or movements, usually without your knowledge or agreement.

SUSTAINABLE DEVELOPMENT GOALS (SDGs) The UN's 17 SDGs are a call for action by all countries to promote prosperity while protecting the planet.

TORTURE The illegal inflicting of severe mental or physical pain or suffering on somebody else.

TRAFFICKING The transport of adults and children in a form of modern slavery, including for sexual exploitation, child labour and forced marriage. It is a global criminal enterprise.

TRANSPHOBIA Discrimination against transgender and non-binary people.

TRAUMA BONDING When an emotional attachment develops between a victim and their abuser.

TREATY A formal agreement in international law between at least two countries.

UNITED NATIONS (UN) An international body formed in 1945 after World War Two, with the goal of bringing all world countries together to work towards world peace, prosperity and human rights.

UNITED NATIONS CONVENTION ON THE RIGHTS OF THE CHILD A legally-binding international agreement setting out the civil, political, economic, social and cultural rights of every child in the world.

VIOLATION The breach of human rights by a government or state.

VOTER A person who votes – or who has the right to vote – in an election, usually in a democratic system.

WHITE SUPREMACY A racist ideology based on the belief that people with white skin are superior and should dominate those with brown or black skin. It extends beyond personal and group attitudes, into the structures of systems and institutions that are designed to support white dominance.

XENOPHOBIA Discrimination based on national identity, for example against refugees and foreigners.

USEFUL ORGANISATIONS

There are many non-governmental organisations (NGOs) that work to support child rights. To find the best ones for you, it's a good idea to start by considering what you really need. Is it expert advice and perhaps someone to whom you can speak confidentially? Are you looking for sources of reliable information? Do you want a safe and effective way to connect with other people?

The list here includes just a few of the many organisations available, so it is best to view them as a starting point and to research others. You can also check if your country has children's rights commissioners. Be aware that in some places NGOs are viewed with suspicion.

INTERNATIONAL

These may have offices in your own country.

- ATD Fourth World International focuses on ending extreme poverty.

- Child Fund Alliance works to end violence and exploitation and to overcome poverty.

- Child Rights Connect is a global network of over 80 organisations. Work includes empowering child rights defenders to influence and use the UN human rights system at national level.

- Consortium for Street Children is a global network dedicated to raising the voices of street-connected children.

- Defence for Children International is a leading international child rights movement, with expertise in the field of criminal justice.

- End Violence Against Children is a global partnership of many organisations working to build a world in which every child grows up safe and secure without fear of violence.

- KidsRights works for a world where all children can access rights. It upholds children as changemakers, and supports the right to voice.

- Malala Fund works to amplify girls' voices and ensure that every girl has access to twelve years of free, safe, quality education.

- Plan International supports child rights and gender equality.

- Restless Development trains, mentors, nurtures and connects young people to lead change.

- Right To Play uses play to protect, educate and empower children and young people.

- Save the Children International champions children's rights and interests.

- Terre des Hommes supports children in need, during war, natural disasters and other situations of distress.

- Theirworld focuses on access to education and skills development.

- United Nations Children's Fund (UNICEF) protects child rights and provides humanitarian and development aid.

- United Nations High Commissioner for Refugees (UNHCR) supports refugees, forcibly displaced communities and stateless people, including children.

- UN Women is the United Nations entity dedicated to gender equality and the empowerment of women and girls.

NATIONAL (UK)

- The Children's Society works for young people facing abuse, exploitation and neglect.

- #iwill champions young people as leaders of change and challenges UK organisations to support youth social action.

- National Society for the Prevention of Cruelty to Children

- National Youth Advocacy Service (NYAS) champions the voices and rights of care experienced children and young people.

NATIONAL (AUSTRALIA & AOTEAROA/ NEW ZEALAND)

- The Centre for Multicultural Youth provides specialist support to Australian young people from migrant and refugee backgrounds.

- Change the Record is Australia's only national Aboriginal-led justice coalition of legal, health and family violence prevention experts.

- Children's Rights Alliance Aotearoa is the collective voice for children's rights in New Zealand

- Olabud Doogethu is an Aboriginal, community-led justice reinvestment site in Western Australia improving outcomes for young people.

- SNAICC works on Aboriginal and Torres Strait Islander children's rights, especially safety, development and well-being.

- Youth Law Australia is a community legal service dedicated to helping children and young people find a legal solution to their problems.

SOURCES

This book includes information originally gathered and published by the following organisations, all of which have useful websites and resources:

- Action Aid
- Amnesty International
- Children's Rights Alliance for England
- Child Rights Now
- Defence for Children International
- Earth Justice
- Equality and Human Rights Commission (UK)
- Food Foundation
- Girls Not Brides
- Global Citizen
- Human Rights First
- Human Rights Watch
- Internal Displacement Monitoring Centre
- International Labour Organisation
- KidsRights

- Minority Rights Group

- National Center for Biotechnology Information (US)

- Office of the High Commissioner for Human Rights, United Nations

- The Open University Children's Research Centre

- Pulitzer Center

- Save the Children

- Small Arms Survey

- Tech Against Trafficking

- UNESCO, United Nations Educational, Scientific and Cultural Organisation

- UNHCR, United Nations High Commissioner for Refugees

- UNICEF, United Nations Children's Fund

- World Bank Identification for Development (ID4D)

- World Health Organisation

- World Organisation Against Torture (OMCT)

- Young People Today

Amnesty International is a global movement of more than 10 million people standing up for humanity and human rights. Our purpose is to protect people wherever justice, fairness, freedom and truth are denied. We are independent of any government, political ideology, economic interest or religion and are funded mainly by our membership and public donations. We work with and for young people on the issues that are most relevant to your lives. You could:

- join or start an Amnesty youth group.

- encourage your teachers to use Amnesty's free human rights education resources, available online.

- if you are in the UK, join Amnesty's Children's Human Rights Network at www.amnesty.org.uk/childrensnetwork

www.amnesty.org.uk
www.amnesty.org.au
www.amnesty.org.nz

ACKNOWLEDGEMENTS: HOW THIS BOOK WAS MADE

This book is the joint creation of many people.

It started with conversations between Angelina Jolie, who has been special envoy to the United Nations High Commission for Refugees for over twenty years and Amnesty International, the world's largest grassroots human rights organisation. We shared a concern that both children and young adults are often unaware of child rights, which can leave you vulnerable and without redress if your rights are not upheld. We also shared a belief in the long-term power of literature to change lives, so we agreed to produce a book. Our goal is for all young people to know and be able to claim your rights, no matter who you are or where you live.

From the outset we were supported by Arminka Helić and Chloe Dalton, who acted as critical friends on the project and to whom we are extremely grateful for their clarity of thought, commitment and integrity.

We were joined by Professor Geraldine Van Bueren QC, an expert in child rights and one of the original drafters of the United Nations Convention on the Rights of the Child, when she represented Amnesty. Together we began to work out our approach.

It was clear that we needed to involve children and young people and do some serious listening. We owe huge thanks to many people.

We are grateful to Mala Tribich, who as a child survived the Holocaust, for her kindness, wisdom and inspiration.

We thank Dr Liz Chamberlain, Dr Trevor Collins and the Open University's Children's Research Centre for invaluable ongoing support. They stepped in and carried out early UK-based research to gather children's ideas and concerns about what needed to go into the book. Their work directly involved 114 children and young people, with a further 100 indirectly involved through a school-based child-led research project. Each project group involved a diverse range of participants, including children from rural communities, urban and peri-urban environments; from low socio-economic backgrounds; from ethnic minority communities; with learning difficulties; from vulnerable groups; and care-experienced children and young people. The

Open University then produced a report based on this research, called *Representing children's rights from discussion through to illustration and interpretation.* We used it to help frame our outline for the book.

For their vital help with the research, we thank: Rose Lloyd and children at Bridges Childcare; Louise Perry and young people at the inclusive theatre Chickenshed; Jill McLachlan and children at Gainford Primary School; Vickie Jones and children at Newlands Primary School; Manya Benenson and young people at Nottingham Playhouse; young care-experienced people via the National Youth Advocacy Service (NYAS) and the Bright Sparks group; Helen Dale at the Observatory on Human Rights of Children, Lleisiau Bach-Little Voices and children of Blaenavon Heritage VC Primary School; Jessica Fermor and children at Seal Primary School; Martin Gallagher, Rhian Parry and Charlotte, Grant, Mick, Myomi, Paris and Tom at St Joseph's Catholic and Anglican High School and Ysgol Rhiwabon, through a partnership with the Travelling Ahead Project and Wrexham Traveller Education Service; and Frances Bestley, director of UNICEF UK's Rights Respecting Schools programme.

Then we went global. We put out the call to all our Amnesty offices in over 70 countries. We invited youth activists in Amnesty's global Youth Power Action Network to comment on the outline and they did – young people from Burkina Faso, Germany, Hong Kong, Ireland, Nigeria and the United States gave us their time and their opinions. We thought hard about everything they said and revised the outline. Then we wrote the first draft and sent it out to global youth and child activists, and also to Amnesty experts on many different human rights areas, including law, research, campaigning, activism and education. Everyone cared and everyone made an input. We took account of everything and revised the manuscript.

Our huge thanks to Casey Dai, Sorcha Kebbe, Miriam Tams and Svenja Wend, Kévine Marie Linda Traore, Tiffany Tse and Zulu Anyaogu from Amnesty's Youth Power Action Network. Also to Vinuki Bakmeedeniya, Michael Quinn and Katherine Walton of the Children's Human Rights Network.

Our special thanks to the amazing activists whose stories are at the heart of this book, all of whom generously gave their consent. In truth, there are many others with powerful stories who deserved to be included, if only we had the space and it were safe to do so. We were constantly mindful of the need to protect young people in some countries and regions.

We are grateful to many colleagues in the Amnesty global movement, chief among them Nathaniel Baverstock, Dora Castillo, Nicky Parker, Bina Patel and Augusta Quiney. We also thank Kate Allen, Clare Bullen, Richard Burton, Iain Byrne, Louise Carmody, May Carolan, Mayda Chan, Chris Chapman, Vongai Chikwanda, Ana Collins, Sara Vida Coumans, Ernest Coverson, Simon Crowther, Oliver Feeley-Sprague, Niki Frencken, Katherine Gerson, Sheila Goncalvez, Saad Hammadi, Saleh Higazi, Tale Longva, Tom Mackey, Jaskiran Kaur Marway, Kerry Moscogiuri, Nicole Millar, Tatiana Movshevich, Cecilia Oluwafisayo Aransiola, Colm O'Gorman, Jess Owen, Kharunya Paramaguru, Katy Pownall, Melody Ross, Merybell Reynoso, Thomas Schulz-Jagow, Renata de Souza, Krittika Vishwanath, Matt Vogel and Jennifer Wells.

We thank our literary agent Stephanie Thwaites of Curtis Brown for being instrumental in bringing our book to life. We are also grateful to Andersen Press for their vision and dedication – we couldn't have wished for a better publishing partner. At Andersen

Press, we thank Paul Black, Kate Grove, Mark Hendle, Sarah Kimmelman, Jack Noel, Chloe Sackur, Charlie Sheppard and Liz White, also the indefatigable Klaus Flugge, himself a child survivor of war, former refugee and long-time friend to Amnesty. Sue Cook's copy-editing skills were invaluable.

Thanks to Mel Larsen for her helpful advice on maintaining a strong approach to equality, diversity and inclusion.

We thank international psychologist Dr Anjhula Mya Singh Bais, who generously gave her time and expertise to advise us on how best to mediate some of the challenging content.

Finally, we acknowledge and thank all the young people around the world bravely working for human rights, and any young person reading this book who is considering joining these efforts.

IMAGE CREDITS

Page 6 Women's strike held in Mexico City to demand the end of violence against women, March 2018. © Itzel Plascencia López/Amnesty International Mexico

8 Holding hands © Pexels

12 Thousands of women take to the streets of Lahore, Pakistan to mark International Women's Day, March 2019. © Ema Anis/Amnesty International

22 A boy rides a bike at a temporary refugee camp in the port area of Thessaloniki, Greece, July 2016. © Richard Burton/Amnesty International

23 Children paint a mural commemorating the life of local chef Nakiea Jackson who was shot dead by police in the kitchen of his restaurant, Kingston, Jamaica, August 2017. © Richard Burton/Amnesty International

26 Students demonstrate on the streets of Uganda's capital Kampala, demanding politicians act urgently in order to prevent further global warming and climate change, May 2019. © Amnesty International

45 Greta Thunberg speaks before accepting the Amnesty International Ambassadors of Conscience Award at the Lisner Auditorium in Washington DC, September 2019. © Andy DelGiudice/Amnesty International

55 LGBTI demonstration in Rio de Janeiro, June 2014. © AF Rodrigues

59 Zulaikha Patel © Reabetswe Mabilo

64 Front row, left to right: disability activists Kane and Jamie. Back row, second left, Jaime, far right, Amy. © Celine Smyth, Swansea University

82 Left to right: Agnesa Murselaj, Amal Azzudin, Roza Salih © PA Images/Alamy Stock Photo

90 Moses Akatugba © Miikka Pirinen/Amnesty Finland

102 Nicole de la Cruz © Amnesty International

104 Left to right: Macrine Akinyi Onyango, Stacy Dina Adhiambo, Cynthia Awuor Otieno, Purity Christine Achieng and Ivy Akinyi

111 Left to right: Janaiya Alfred, Gabriel Kizer

124 Magai Matiop Ngong © Amnesty International

140 Tokata Iron Eyes speaks at the Amnesty International Ambassadors of Conscience Award at the Lisner Auditorium in Washington DC, September 2019. © Andy DelGiudice/Amnesty International

142 Dujuan Hoosan © Jonny Rowden

150 Malala Yousafzai at Amnesty International's Ambassador of Conscience Awards 2013 celebrations in Dublin, Ireland. © Joao Pina/MAPS Images

158 Said shown at back, arms raised. © Right To Play

163 Zlata Filipović © Dragana Jurisic

171 Annie Alfred © LAWILINK/Amnesty International

173 Top, left to right: André Oliveira, Sofia Oliveira © Nuno Gaspar Oliveira
Bottom, left to right: Cláudia Duarte, Martim Duarte, Mariana Duarte, Catarina Mota. © André Mota

176 March in support of the missing Ayotzinapa students, Mexico City, October 2014. © Alonso Garibay/Amnesty International Mexico

183 Left to right: climate activists Vanessa Nakate, Luisa Neubauer, Greta Thunberg, Isabelle Axelsson and Loukina Tille at a news conference in Davos, Switzerland, 24 January 2020. Vanessa Nakate was initially cropped out of the photo, provoking an international debate on diversity and erasure. © Markus Schreiber/AP/Shutterstock

195 Amnesty Netherlands supporters and members take part in Write for Rights events in Amsterdam, December 2020. © Karen Veldkamp

199 Amnesty International activists during the preparations of an action on the Greek island of Lesbos, July 2017. © Giorgos Moutafis/Amnesty International

201 Write for Rights school event in support of land rights campaigner Nonhle Mbuthuma, December 2018. © Amnesty International South Africa

204 Fridays for Future movement activists from the Philippines, May 2019. © Nichol Francis Anduyan

210 A global petition to reform the Finnish Trans Act is handed to Secretary of State Paula Lehtomäki by trans activist Sakris Kupila, March 2017. © Tomi Asikainen/Amnesty International

217 Women's strike held in Mexico City to demand the end of violence against women, March 2018. © Itzel Plascencia López/Amnesty International Mexico

218 Amnesty International Benin Letter Writing event, part of Amnesty's annual Write for Rights Campaign, December 2020. © Amnesty International

220 Women's march in Kyiv, Ukraine, March 2020. © Amnesty International Ukraine

225 Over 40 representatives from the Grassy Narrows community demonstrate in Toronto, Canada, June 2019. © Allan Lissner

226 Protestors face off with riot police guarding the house of Jaroslaw Kaczynski, leader of Poland's ruling Law and Justice party (PIS) during a demonstration against a decision by the Constitutional Court on abortion law restriction, in Warsaw, October 2020. © Grzegorz Żukowski

237 Amnesty Germany activists protest as Egyptian president Fattah Al-Sisi meets with German chancellor Angela Merkel in Berlin, October 2018. © Henning Schacht/Amnesty International

239 Climate justice advocate Marinel Ubaldo © Eloisa Lopez/Amnesty International

243 Left to right: climate activists Ranton Anjain, Litokne Kabua, David Ackley III, Carlos Manuel, Carl Smith

246 Amnesty Taiwan activists pasting Liu Xiaobo and Liu Xia graphics on graffiti walls by Riverside Park, Taipei, July 2017. © Amnesty International Taiwan

All other images of activists reproduced with their permission.

Every effort has been made to gain approval from rights holders and informed consent from the individuals whose stories are featured in this book. All information has been checked and approved by experts at the time of going to print, but some facts and figures may change thereafter.

NOTES